Structural Adjustment in sub-Saharan Africa

90 0587259 3

Structural Adjustment in sub-Saharan Africa

Robert Lensink

Longman
London and New York

Longman Group UK Limited,
Longman House, Burnt Mill,
Harlow, Essex CM20 2JE, England
and Associated Companies throughout the world.

*Published in the United States of America
by Longman Publishing, New York*

First published 1996

ISBN 0 582 248868 PPR

British Library Cataloguing-in-Publication Data

A catalogue record for this book is
available from the British Library

Library of Congress Cataloging-in-Publication Data

A catalog record for this book is
available from the Library of Congress

Set by 8 in 10/12 Times
Produced through Longman Malaysia, LWP

Contents

Tables

Acknowledgements

My intention of writing this book developed in 1993 when I started to give some seminars on structural adjustments in sub-Saharan Africa, both at the University of Ouagadougou, in Burkina Faso, and the University of Groningen, in the Netherlands. Students of both universities are gratefully acknowledged for their very stimulating remarks.

I am also indebted to many friends and colleagues for their invaluable help in preparing this text. I express my gratitude especially to Nanne Brunia, Niels Hermes, Caroline Jongkamp, Ger Lanjouw, Clemens Lutz, Victor Murinde and Caspar Schweigman for their willingness to comment on preliminary versions of different parts of this book. Their suggestions considerably improved this work.

Special thanks are devoted to Rients Abma and Focco Vijselaar. Rients and Focco assisted me, during different time periods, in writing the book. The work I did with Focco actually forms the basis of Chapter 7. Moreover, Focco did a lot of preliminary work for several other chapters as well, especially with respect to Chapters 4 and 5. Rients was willing to read the entire manuscript and to check for inconsistencies, typing errors and lack of clarities.

I am particularly grateful for the English translation made by Ingrid Hadders.

Last, but not least, I would like to thank Ans Braam for her patience, friendship and love. Without her mental support this book would never have been finished.

1 Introduction and survey

Since the early 1980s many developing countries in sub-Saharan Africa – henceforth Africa – have experienced an economic depression. This depression manifests itself in a decreasing per capita income, an increase in foreign debts and an increase in government deficits. Furthermore, most African countries have to contend with inefficient production processes and inadequate institutions. Africa's poor economic development is neither a recent nor a temporary phenomenon. Already from the end of the 1960s onwards there has been a decrease in economic growth. This downward tendency continued during the 1980s. To provide an answer to these disequilibria and imperfections, the World Bank introduced adjustment loans which were to finance reform programmes for the entire economy or a specific sector of the economy. An important element of these adjustment loans are the conditions regarding policy – i.e. conditionalities – the World Bank has attached to the possibility to make use of the credit facilities. For a long time the International Monetary Fund (IMF) has had a considerable influence by means of stabilisation loans on policies in developing countries faced with economic difficulties. At present in almost all African countries stabilisation and structural adjustment programmes have been put into effect; the programmes are very much determined by the World Bank and IMF conditionalities.

This book offers an overview of the debate on the adjustment programmes in Africa as financed by the World Bank and the IMF. Attention will be paid both to theoretical arguments with respect to the economic point of view underlying the adjustment programmes and to the practical contents and effects of the adjustment programmes in Africa. Because of the crucial role that the World Bank and the IMF play in introducing adjustment programmes, a lot of attention is paid to the basic principles of these two institutions. The viewpoints of the critics of the World Bank and the IMF will also be discussed.

In order to study structural adjustments it is essential to have an understanding of economic theory. Characteristic of this book is that structural adjustments in Africa will be approached by comparing the viewpoints of neoliberals and those of structuralists. During the past decades these theories have been predominant in debates on development. The neoliberals, who mainly base their case on neoclassical theory, argue in favour of a policy aimed at the improvement of the market mechanism. The structuralists, on the other hand, are advocates of government intervention. The World Bank and the IMF are influenced by neoliberals to a large extent, whereas critics of the World Bank and the IMF mainly refer to the structuralists.

Before I continue to discuss the contents of the various chapters of this book, a brief outline will be given of the evolution of development theories and strategies since the Second World War.

1.1 The period prior to the structural adjustments

The policy conditions imposed by the IMF and World Bank with respect to structural adjustments mainly refer to improving the market mechanism, decreasing government intervention, and a free trade policy. Countries have to open up to competition from the world market. The current emphasis on improving market forces is in sharp contrast with the development policies as they were pursued in most developing countries during the first decade after the Second World War. During that period market pessimism and the advantages of government intervention dominated the debate on the development policy to pursue. The development policy during this period of time was characterised by an emphasis on large-scale industrialisation, heavy government intervention, and a trade policy aimed at protecting the domestic economy against competition on the world market. This policy is theoretically supported by a number of trail-blazing articles in the development literature which Roemer and Radelet (1991) divided into three groups:

- balanced and unbalanced growth
- the inferior role of the agricultural sector
- literature on trade.

Balanced and unbalanced growth

The first group consists of literature concerned with the pros and cons of balanced versus unbalanced growth. The theory of balanced economic growth emphasises the importance of a minimum volume of the investment programme, also known as the Big Push (Rosenstein–Rodan, 1943), and the importance of balanced development of the various sectors of the economy (see e.g. Nurkse, 1953). The underlying notion is that a simultaneous development of different sectors that produce different goods will lead to a market that has reached such a size that there is enough employment and purchasing power to start a process of economic development. Paramount in this theory are the complementarities which refer to the fact that different economic activities have a stimulating effect on each other. These complementarities are divided into complementarities of demand, complementarities of infrastructure, and complementarities in production (Myint, 1980, Ch. 7; Szirmai, 1994, Ch. 7). The complementarities of demand refer to the significance of purchasing power. Several factories must be developed simultaneously since the products made in one factory can be sold only if the employees of the other factory earn enough money to buy these products. If there is just one factory in an otherwise traditional economy, the purchasing power will be too small to guarantee the sales of the factory. The complementarities of infrastructure refer to the importance of a good infrastructure to the transport of raw materials and final goods. A poor infrastructure will hamper the development of the industry to a great extent. Complementarities in production refer to companies selling products to each other, such as raw materials. In extreme cases the theory of balanced growth argues in favour of an extensively integrated industrialisation programme which simultaneously develops and stimulates the consumer goods industry as well as the infrastructure and the capital goods industry. This mutual stimulation is brought about by the connections between the various sectors. Government planning is essential since the market itself cannot produce such incentives for investment.

The advocates of unbalanced growth, too (e.g. Hirschman, 1958) stress the significance of the relation between different sectors. Paramount are the so-called forward and backward linkages. A forward linkage occurs when the availability of a particular product encourages investment in a different production process. Thus, the food processing industry may be stimulated by the presence of agricultural products. A backward linkage refers to the fact that a particular economic activity can take place only if inputs are supplied by other enterprises. The theory of unbalanced growth distinguishes between weak and strong linkages. With respect to the above, the theory points to the strong backward linkage between industry and infrastructure; a flourishing industry requires an excellent infrastructure. On the other hand, the forward linkage between infrastructure and industry is minor; infrastructure makes industry possible but is not indispensable (Szirmai, 1994, p. 229).

Advocates of unbalanced growth and advocates of balanced growth come to different conclusions. According to the advocates of unbalanced growth, a process of economic development is actually maintained by imbalances. Economic policy should focus on several strategic sectors that show many strong linkages to other sectors. When these key sectors have been developed or stimulated, a process of economic development is brought about by the technical relationships between these and other sectors of the economy. Advocates of unbalanced growth too argue in favour of planning and government intervention albeit in a smaller degree than advocates of the theory of balanced growth.

The inferior role of the agricultural sector

The second group stresses the inferior role of the agricultural sector in the process of economic development. It is stated that the agricultural sector, as compared to the industrial sector, is less productive and has fewer linkages to other economic sectors. Moreover, according to the supporters of this view, smallholders tend to be rather traditional and insensitive to market swings. On the basis of the above, government interventions are argued in favour of, with a view to stimulating the industrial sector at the expense of the agricultural sector. The government has to stimulate labourers who used to be active in the agricultural sector to be deployed in the industrial sector.

With respect to this view, Lewis' (1954) opinions in particular are a significant starting-point. Lewis (1954) developed an economic model which consists of a traditional, overpopulated rural sector and a modern, urban industrial sector. According to Lewis, labour migration from the traditional rural sector to the modern urban sector has a positive effect on the economy because the fact that these labourers leave the rural sector will not lead to a decreasing agricultural production due to the surplus of labour in this sector. This surplus of labour in the agricultural sector results in a situation where too many labourers work on too small a piece of land which results in a marginal productivity of labour that equals zero in this sector. This implies that the agricultural production does not decrease as a result of one labourer abandoning the agricultural sector for the industrial sector. The production of this labourer can easily be taken over by the remaining labourers in the agricultural sector due to the existence of disguised unemployment. Labourers who migrate from the agricultural to the industrial sector will settle for much lower wages since they are used to living at the subsistence level. Thus companies in the industrial sector are able to make a profit which will finance new investment and initiate a process of economic development.

Literature on trade

The third group refers to the literature on trade. An inward-oriented development strategy is advocated. Such a strategy stresses the need for the development of a domestic industry that produces for the domestic market and that is protected against competition from the world market. There are several reasons for the above (Greenaway and Milner, 1993, Ch. 3).

First, developing countries are said to be faced with a structural decrease in the terms of trade. The terms of trade measures the price a country receives for its exports in relation to the price a country has to pay for its imports. A fall in the terms of trade implies that a country will have to export more goods in order to be able to import the same amount of goods. The starting-point is that developing countries would be forced to export primary goods (agricultural products and raw materials) if they were to open up to competition from the world market whereas developed countries would apply themselves to producing manufactured goods. According to the supporters of this line of reasoning, the demand for products from developing countries will lag behind to a fairly large degree during the process of development in which the income in developed countries will increase. Studies have been trying to find an explanation for this in the allegedly low income elasticity of the demand for primary goods. Income elasticity measures the percentage change in demand for a product due to a percentage change in income. If income elasticity is low, an increase in income will only slightly affect the demand for the product concerned in a positive manner. In time, in comparison to the income elasticity of the demand for manufactured goods, the low income elasticity of the demand for primary goods leads to the prices of primary goods being influenced negatively in relation to the prices of manufactured goods (the Singer–Prebisch theorem).

Second, developing countries are said to be faced with great instability of the prices of their exports. With respect to this argument too, the basic idea is that developing countries will export primary products. In this particular context, however, the emphasis is on the fact that the price elasticity of the demand for primary goods is very small. Price elasticity measures the effect of a percentage change of the price on the percentage change of the demand for certain goods. In relation to the considerable fluctuations in the supply of primary goods on the world market due to the possibility of crop failure, small price elasticity leads to fluctuating prices on the world market. For if the production increases (decreases) globally, a balance of supply and demand on the world market requires a considerable reduction (increase) of prices on the world market since the demand for goods is only affected by price movements to some extent. If the price elasticity of demand were substantial, a surplus supply of goods might be dealt with by means of a slight reduction of prices since price reduction consequently will lead to a great increase in the demand.

Third, there is the infant industry argument. Usually industries in developing countries are rather underdeveloped or do not even exist. Due to economies of scale and the consequently lower costs industries from the developed world are faced with, industries in developing countries may not be able to survive unless they are protected for a certain period of time. Therefore, short-term protection of domestic industries against competition from highly developed industries from the developed world is argued in favour of.

Finally, attention is being paid to the unfair distribution of the advantages of trade. Especially the centre-periphery concept by Prebisch (1950) provided the foundation for this notion. In this theory, international trade leads to an increasing dependence of the periphery (the developing countries) on the centre (the developed countries), and profits from trade very much flow to the centre. The theory states that the initial inequality between the developed and the developing countries is fed by trade. If developed countries have an initial advantage in producing goods that require large amounts of capital (machines), or if developed countries have an initial advantage producing goods that are technologically highly developed, trade will lead to the production process in the developed countries becoming increasingly capital-intensive or of a technologically higher quality. However, in developing countries which have an initial advantage with respect to unskilled labour, trade will stimulate the production of goods which require unskilled labour. If this is considered in connection with the unfavourable development of the terms of trade of primary goods – the production of which most often requires unskilled labour – trade will lead to stagnation in developing countries.

The above-mentioned theoretical views have greatly influenced postwar economic policies. Structuralism used to be the prevailing development strategy and theory. The term structuralism was first used by a group of economists who worked at the United Nations Economic Commission for Latin America (ECLA). These economists stressed the peripheral status of Latin America as compared to the capitalist centre, and the heterogeneous structure of the Latin American economies which were characterised by different levels of development of the various sectors (Jenkins, 1992, p. 136). In the course of time the term structuralism was used in a much broader context. Today structuralism refers to a number of theories that react against the orthodox neoliberal lines of reasoning. In this book the term 'structuralism' refers to a large group of economists, ranging from Marxists to moderate social democrats who share the following basic principles (see also Jenkins, 1992):

1 The advantages of the free market are criticised. Structuralists stress the existence of market imperfections which government intervention should overcome, and the existing fundamental difference between developed and developing countries. Structuralists doubt the fact that economic subjects respond strongly to price incentives.
2 An emphasis on structural changes. Development is regarded as a process of transformation of economic and social structures in an economy; in this process industrialisation plays an important role.
3 The role of ownership distribution. Structuralists stress the fact that a concentration of ownership with a small group of people has a significant influence on economic development. Therefore, an analysis of ownership distribution is very important to the understanding of the process of development.
4 The significant role of capital accumulation. Structuralists feel that an increase in capital accumulation (investment in machines) is crucial to an increasing economic growth.

African economic policy was influenced by structuralist points of view to a great extent. Thus, a stylised description of policies in Africa might include six points. First, trade policy is not directed towards exports. A policy of import substitution is advocated for the purpose of stimulating the domestic industry. In this context import and export quotas, taxes on exports, and tariffs are frequently used. As a result the agricultural sector, which traditionally used to be the exporting sector, is put at a great disadvantage in comparison with the industrial sector. Second, the government regulates international currency transactions. The government determines the exchange rate; international capital transactions are limited; currencies are non-convertible; and the government distributes the existing amount of international currencies among those sectors and companies they wish to support. Third, the domestic financial market is very much influenced by government regulation. The authorities try to stimulate economic development by determining interest ceilings, by subsidising credit to targeted sectors, and by encouraging banks to make financial means available to certain sectors. As a result few financial institutions exist in agricultural areas. Fourth, the labour market is highly influenced by the government. In many cases the government determines minimum wages, and the government makes it quite impossible to fire people by means of regulations. Fifth, to a great extent prices of goods are determined or influenced by government policy. Finally, the government has a strong influence through state-owned enterprises (mining, oil), marketing organisations in agricultural sectors, and many semi-governmental enterprises.

From the early 1980s onwards much more emphasis has been placed on the advantages of a free market mechanism and thus on a moderation of government intervention. The neoliberal point of view was widely accepted. This viewpoint is based on three principles (Jenkins, 1992, p. 161):

1 Individualism: individuals instead of social structures are paramount in neoliberal analyses.
2 The significance of free markets: neoliberals presuppose that markets function well, and that these initiate the efficient allocation of production factors. Property rights are neglected. The private sector should be able to function in an environment where there is free competition, and an outward-oriented development strategy is preferred to a strategy that is inward-oriented.
3 Flexibility: contrary to the structuralists – who emphasise the existence of structural rigidities in developing countries – the neoliberals assume that there is a great amount of flexibility. According to the neoliberals both producers and consumers respond strongly to price incentives. According to the neoliberals, smallholders in developing countries also act as rational, economically maximising persons so that in these situations economic incentives will also have the desired effects (see e.g. Schultz, 1964). It is supposed that an increase in prices of agricultural products leads to an increase in agricultural production. Moreover, a productive agricultural sector is considered to be an essential feature of the development process.

An important reason for the present-day emphasis on neoliberal principles is the changing intellectual climate in the West. Neoconservatism – which centres around neoliberal notions – became widely accepted. The good economic results of rather outward-oriented developing countries, like South Korea, Singapore and Hong Kong, compared to the results of inwardly focusing developing countries also play a part in this change. With respect to the above, strong economic progress in these countries is often wrongly associated with less government intervention. A significant argument in favour of the importance attached to a free market mechanism can also be found in those theoretical and empirical studies that point to the great disadvantages of a protectionist policy and the advantages of an outward-oriented development strategy (see Balassa, 1982; Krueger, 1978).

1.2 The structure of this book

The IMF and the World Bank gave a sympathetic ear to the neoliberal notions; thus, the adjustment programmes developed by these institutions were inspired by neoliberalism. Most African countries, when confronted with great economic difficulties and a lack of means to overcome them, were more or less forced to use the credit facilities provided by the IMF and the World Bank for reforming their economies.

This book centres around the structural adjustments in Africa during the 1980s. The analysis begins with a macroeconomic description of Africa (Chapter 2). In view of this description an attempt will be made to present a stylised macroeconomic picture of an average African country. Africa will be compared with several other regions of developing countries. Furthermore, several African countries will be discussed separately. In Chapter 3 attention will be paid to the causes of the economic crisis in Africa; in this context both the views of the neoliberal economists and the views of the structuralists will be discussed in accordance with the above distinction. Moreover, Chapter 3 also presents a survey of a number of recent empirical studies into the causes of the African crisis. Next, three consecutive chapters present a detailed account of the role of the IMF and the World Bank in those structural adjustments in Africa. When the IMF and the World Bank were founded, responsibilities were clearly divided between the two institutions. When the adjustment loans were introduced in the 1980s, the institutions started to move in on each other's sphere of activity. Structural adjustment programmes in most African countries were designed by the IMF in cooperation with the World Bank, so that it is rather difficult to distinguish between the IMF and the World Bank contributions. Chapter 6, which concentrates on the conditionalities in the adjustment programmes, does not distinguish between the IMF and the World Bank. Chapters 4 and 5 will discuss the IMF and the World Bank separately. These chapters describe the structure of the two institutions and their credit facilities for financing adjustments. Furthermore, attention will be paid to the theoretical background of the stabilisation and structural adjustment programmes by the IMF and the World Bank. Chapter 7 presents a survey of the studies that analyse the economic effects of the structural adjustment programmes by the IMF and the World Bank. Despite numerous problems that arise when evaluating adjustment programmes and the different methods of evaluating, judgement can be passed on the economic results of the programmes, albeit somewhat cautiously. In the course of time the adjustment programmes by the IMF and the World Bank have met their critics halfway to a certain extent. However, there are still some very significant differences between the approach of these two multilateral institutions and the approach of their critics. In Chapter 8 attention will be paid to criticism of the adjustment programmes. Aspects that will be dealt with are, for example, the effect of adjustment programmes on the role of women, poverty, and the environment. Moreover, an alternative adjustment programme is presented in accordance with structuralist views. Chapter 9 will provide a summary of the issues discussed and point at some relevant future research issues with respect to structural adjustment.

2 A macroeconomic outline of Africa

Sub-Saharan Africa consists of the entire African continent south of the Sahara with the exception of South Africa. Sub-Saharan Africa comprises about forty-five countries with extremely varying populations. Some countries have a population of over 50 million, like Ethiopia and Nigeria, and a great number of small countries have fewer than a million inhabitants, for example Cape Verde, Swaziland and the Seychelles. The average population is just over 10 million. The political situations in these countries differ strongly. In some countries no political parties are allowed (Sierra Leone, Sudan and Somalia) whereas in other countries there is only one political party (Swaziland and Uganda); in Nigeria and Djibouti the number of authorised political parties is limited whereas the remaining countries are officially characterised by a multiparty system (van der Kraaij, 1994, Table 3.4).

Despite great differences the economic problems of these countries are comparable. Most African countries are characterised by an extremely low per capita income, little or sometimes even negative growth of per capita income, high population growth, a lack of basic facilities with respect to health care and education, poor infrastructure and an unstable political situation. Furthermore, many countries were struck by the debt crisis and environmental problems, such as deforestation. The African countries are among the poorest countries of the world, which means that the majority of the Least Developed Countries (LLDCs) is situated on this continent.[1] Table A2.1 (see Appendix 1 to this chapter) presents an overview of some macroeconomic and social data of individual African countries.

This chapter presents a macroeconomic survey of Africa. The macroeconomic description centres mostly around the regions that are relevant to the adjustment programmes. The structure of this chapter is based on the interpretations of a number of macroeconomic identities (see Appendix 2 to this chapter). The chapter starts with a description of the African production process; in this context the development of growth and the structure of production in Africa will be discussed. Next, attention will be paid to international trade which, to a great extent, is influenced by the growth and structure of domestic production. An improvement of domestic production can be accomplished by increasing investment. The development of investment will be discussed in Section 2.3. Investment is financed with domestic and foreign savings, the development of which will be discussed in three consecutive sections. Domestic savings are paramount in Section 2.4. An explicit distinction is made between savings of the private sector and government savings. Foreign savings consist of foreign capital flows and interest payments on foreign debts. Section 2.5 will deal with the development of foreign capital flows to Africa. Section 2.6 discusses the debt crisis. The summary in Section 2.7 concludes this chapter.

Analysing the data, one ought to keep in mind the poor quality of the African data available. In many countries the process of collecting and processing data is rather underdeveloped. Many data are not available, which makes it rather difficult to actually prove certain views. Thus, significant differences in views are allowed to remain existent. Moreover, quite often differences appear to exist between data supplied by different publishing institutions. Finally, statistics are most often restricted to the formal sector. In general the activities of the so-called informal sector are not included in macroeconomic data. Since the African informal sector is a dynamic one responsible for a substantial share of total production and employment, abstracting from these data may result in too negative a picture. Moreover, many activities in Africa relate to subsistence production, or production which is not traded on the market. One tries to include the value of subsistence production in data on gross domestic product (GDP) or gross national product (GNP).[2] However, there is a considerable margin of error in estimating subsistence production, so that the GDP or GNP figures should be taken with caution (see Appendix 1 of this chapter for a discussion on the use of GNP figures). Despite the above restrictions I have tried to substantiate matters with statistics as much as possible. The analysis has been performed at a high aggregate level, though. The average situation in Africa is compared to the averages in other developing regions. This does not do justice to the existing differences between countries. In order to somewhat meet this problem, I shall also discuss the points of interest distinguished with reference to some atypical African countries – data availability permitting, that is. Furthermore, six countries (Ghana, the Ivory Coast, Kenya, Madagascar, Nigeria and Tanzania) have been selected to which special attention will be paid. Ghana, the Ivory Coast, Kenya, Madagascar, Nigeria and Tanzania were among the first countries to carry through IMF and World Bank adjustment programmes. Furthermore, the population of these countries amounts to over 10 million, which means that they are among the relatively large countries of Africa. Data availability was also an important reason for selecting these six countries. Some 'problem' countries like Ethiopia, Mozambique, Sudan and Uganda – also countries with a relatively high population – could not be included in the analysis of individual countries due to a lack of data.

2.1 Production: a crisis in the agricultural and industrial sector

The poor economic development of Africa is reflected by an average annual growth rate of GDP during the 1980–92 period of about 2 per cent, whereas the growth rate of East and South Asia was about 8 and 5 per cent respectively (Table 2.1).[3] The average annual growth rate of Africa equals the annual growth rate in Latin America, but there population growth is much lower. Per capita growth of GDP in the different regions of developing countries is lowest in Africa.

Despite better growth figures in the period before 1980, poor economic development in Africa is neither a recent nor a temporary phenomenon (Abbott, 1993, p. 5). The average growth rate of GDP was about 4 per cent during the 1970–80 period. However, this is very much the result of a relatively high growth during the early 1970s, which is shown by the 1973–80 average growth rate. During this period average growth was only 2.5 per cent whereas it was 6 per cent during the 1965–73 period (World Bank, 1989, Table 2).

Since the late 1960s there has been decreasing economic growth. This downward tendency continued through the 1980s although there seems to have been a slight improvement since the late 1980s.[4] The same pattern can be discerned in the six countries selected: the growth rate decreased from the end of the 1960s onwards. An exception is Ghana which experienced higher growth during the 1980s than during the 1970s. However, in the case of Ghana the following applies: growth was higher during the 1960s, and present-day growth of GDP is low in comparison to population growth. In the 1980s Kenya developed relatively favourably whereas Nigeria, Madagascar and especially the Ivory Coast stand out in a rather negative way. The situation with respect to Nigeria does seem to be improving: since 1988 the annual growth rate of GDP has been over 5 per cent (World Bank, 1993b, Table 6).

GDP is very much determined by the agricultural sector in Africa (Table 2.2). In Tanzania the share of the agricultural sector in GDP is even over 50 per cent. To many African countries agricultural products like corn, coconuts, earthnuts, legumes, sugar and cotton are essential. Only in very small countries, such as Botswana, Gabon, Namibia, Mauritius, Congo, Cape Verde and Leshoto, the share of the agricultural sector in GDP is less than 15 per cent (World Bank, 1993a, p. 243).

In Africa the share of the agricultural sector in GDP showed a downward tendency

Table 2.1 Average annual growth of production (per cent)

	GDP		Industry		Agriculture	
	1970–80	1980–92	1970–80	1980–92	1970–80	1980–92
Africa	3.6	1.8	3.6	1.2	1.6	1.7
East Asia	6.6	7.7	9.4	9.4	3.1	4.4
South Asia	3.5	5.2	4.6	6.4	1.8	3.3
Latin America	5.4	1.8	5.7	1.3	3.4	2.0
Ghana	−0.1	3.4	−1.0	4.0	−0.3	1.2
Ivory Coast	6.8	0.0	9.1	4.4	2.7	−1.0
Kenya	6.4	4.0	8.6	3.9	4.8	2.9
Madagascar	0.5	1.1	0.6	0.8	0.4	2.4
Nigeria	4.6	2.3	7.3	0.2	−0.1	3.6
Tanzania	3.0	3.1	2.6	2.2	0.7	3.8

Source: World Bank, 1993a; 1994b, Table 2

since the 1960s when this share was 43 per cent. Despite the fact that the agricultural share in the process of development decreases in most countries, this tendency is not per definition favourable to Africa. Today the share of the labour force active in the agricultural sector is very large: varying between 50 and 90 per cent (World Bank, 1990a). Moreover, many economists consider an increasing agricultural production to be a prerequisite for raising the African standard of living. The agricultural sector should meet the needs of the growing population and prevent food imports. Furthermore, the agricultural sector has to create jobs for the increasing labour force and by means of exporting it has to provide the required amount of foreign currency. The World Bank (1989, p. 89) argues that a 4 per cent increase of the agricultural production is required to achieve these objectives. In this context the low average growth figures of the agricultural production both during the 1970s and the 1980s are quite alarming (Table 2.1). What is promising, however, is the fact that Tanzania, Madagascar, Ghana and Nigeria have recently managed to realise a higher growth of agricultural production, although growth in these countries is still below the desired minimum growth as defined by the World Bank.

On the entire African continent the share of industrial production is higher than the share of agricultural production. Yet, to most individual countries the industrial sector is of minor importance. The high average is determined to a great extent by Nigeria which shows a 38 per cent share. During the 1980s the average annual growth of industrial production amounted to a mere 1 per cent (Table 2.1). In this respect again, economic crises were not recent phenomena. Although during the 1970s growth was about 4 per cent, this was still in stark contrast with the average growth rate of 14 per cent of the late 1960s (World Bank, 1989, Table 2). The high growth rate of industrial production during the 1960s was a direct result of the economic policy in Africa which very much favoured the industrial sector over the agricultural sector. These problems are not recent ones which is proven by the fact that already during the 1970s the increasing production of manufactured goods – the most dynamic section of industrialised production – was negative in the African LLDCs (World Bank, 1989, p. 110). This tendency continued until the 1980s.

2.2 Trade: little diversification

The previous section showed that both agricultural and industrial production in Africa have a low average growth rate. The crisis in the industrial sector and especially the one in the agricultural sector resulted in stagnating export growth. However, note that the relation can also be the other way round. Poor growth results may be caused by poor export results. In the early 1980s there was actually negative export growth (Elbadawi *et al.*, 1992, p. 12). More recently the situation has improved somewhat. Still, export growth is low in comparison with other regions (Table 2.3). The low growth rate of exports during the 1980s is in contrast with the development of exports in the 1960s. During that period export growth in Africa was substantial compared to other developing countries (Elbadawi *et al.*, 1992, p. 12). In the 1970s, however,

Table 2.2 Structure of production (share in GDP)

	Agriculture 1970	Agriculture 1992	Industry 1970	Industry 1992
Africa	27	20	28	34
East Asia	34	21	34	38
South Asia	44	32	21	26
Latin America	12	–	36	–
Ghana	47	49	18	16
Ivory Coast	40	37	23	23
Kenya	33	27	20	19
Madagascar	24	33	16	14
Nigeria	41	37	14	38
Tanzania	41	61	17	12

Source: World Bank, 1993a; 1994b, Table 3

export growth was already much lower than in most other developing regions. In Ghana, export growth was relatively high in the 1980s whereas growth of exports in Tanzania, Madagascar and Nigeria was low. The great improvement in Ghanian export growth during the 1980s is rather striking and corresponds with the growing GDP in Ghana, which was already noted in the previous section.

The low import growth rate in Africa is caused by, among other things, poor export results (Table 2.3). Exports provide a country with the opportunity of earning foreign currencies which are necessary for importing goods and services. The growth rate of African import is very much influenced by the extremely bad situation in Nigeria where imports decrease by no less than 10 per cent per year. The situation in Nigeria also partly explains the relatively high average imports in Africa in the 1970s; in Nigeria the increase in imports was rather substantial during this period of time. Nigeria's importing and exporting behaviour is the result of the steeply rising oil prices – oil being Nigeria's most important export product – in the late 1970s and the early 1980s and the extreme drop of oil prices after 1985. To Nigeria the falling of oil prices means that Nigeria has to increase exports of oil or other goods in order to be able to pay for imports. Thus the overall picture for Africa, including Nigeria, is not very promising.

The relatively low growth rate of exports resulted in a considerable decrease in the share of African exports in the total global exports. From the 1960s onwards Africa lost more than half of its share in total world exports. The share of primary goods – especially agricultural products – in total exports is very large (Table 2.4). Therefore, to a great extent the disappointing results of the export sector can be traced back to the meagre results of agricultural exports.

The structure of African exports is of significance to the long-term prospects. In Africa the structure of exports hardly changed since the early 1960s, contrary to the situation in other developing regions. In these regions the share of primary goods in

Table 2.3 Average annual growth of exports and imports (per cent)

	Exports 1970–80	Exports 1980–92	Imports 1970–80	Imports 1980–91
Africa	2.8	2.4	3.0	−2.7
East Asia	9.5	10.5	7.8	8.8
South Asia	3.6	6.8	2.7	2.1
Latin America	−0.1	2.9	3.6	0.6
Ghana	−6.3	8.0	−2.2	1.8
Ivory Coast	4.7	7.6	9.1	1.1
Kenya	2.9	4.1	1.9	−1.0
Madagascar	−3.0	−1.6	−0.8	−1.5
Nigeria	0.4	1.7	19.4	−10.5
Tanzania	−7.5	−1.2	−0.6	−1.3

Source: World Bank, 1994b, Table 13

Table 2.4 Structure of exports and imports (share in total exports and imports)

	Primary exports 1970	Primary exports 1992	Manufactured imports 1970	Manufactured imports 1992
Africa	83	76	80	76
East Asia	67	26	70	75
South Asia	53	27	55	61
Latin America	88	62	71	75
Ghana	99	99	70	57
Ivory Coast	94	90	77	59
Kenya	87	71	80	75
Madagascar	93	81	78	75
Nigeria	98	99	85	77
Tanzania	87	85	82	76

Source: World Bank, 1994b, Tables 14 and 15

the total exports dropped substantially. The share of primary goods in the African exports is about 80 per cent (Table 2.4). Exports in most countries consist of agricultural products, and frequently only a few products make up the main constituent of these exports. For Africa the export of bananas, cocoa, coffee, cotton, earthnuts, rubber, sugar, tea and tobacco is of major importance. Therefore, the fact that the African share in world exports of most of the products relevant to Africa has dropped significantly since the 1960s is rather alarming (Table 2.5). The Asian countries improved their share in the world export of these products. The situation in Nigeria is different from that in the other African countries. There are only a few countries – Sierra Leone, Benin, the Central African Republic and Zimbabwe – where manufactured goods make up a significant part of the exports.

Since 1970 the structure of African imports hardly changed (Table 2.4). For years manufactured goods made up the most important part of imports. The share of food imports is small. A detailed study of the composition of African imports shows that a large part of the African imports consists of capital goods and intermediate goods (Lopez and Rodrik, 1989, p. 1). Since these goods are of great importance to the production, it is essential to Africa to increase or at least maintain a certain level of the imports of these goods. This is also confirmed by the relatively rigid production structure with hardly any possibilities for substituting imported means of production for domestic means of production. For example, a decrease in imports of machinery will directly lead to a decrease in production. Imported machinery cannot be substituted for machinery that has been produced at home since this machinery does not have the required quality or simply because it is not produced at home.

2.3 Limited volume and low efficiency of investment

An increase in production of both the industrial and the agricultural sector requires, among other things, an increase in the productivity of capital or an increase in capital stock.

Table 2.5 The most important African articles for export (share in world exports)

	1961–69	1970–79	1980–89	1988–90
Bananas	9.0	5.9	2.9	2.8
Cocoa	67.4	59.6	47.4	44.5
Coffee	24.5	27.1	21.9	19.2
Cotton	12.1	12.8	10.9	12.9
Earthnuts	61.1	39.0	18.4	20.4
Rubber	6.9	5.6	5.1	6.1
Sugar	5.7	4.5	4.5	5.2
Tea	8.7	14.9	15.3	14.9
Tobacco	9.4	8.5	10.1	12.5
Total	17.9	17.7	14.8	13.9
Agriculture	7.1	5.7	3.7	2.9
Trade	2.7	2.4	1.6	1.2

Source: Akiyama and Larson, 1994

Notes: 'Total' is the total of the nine products as a share in total world exports of these articles. 'Agriculture' is the share of agricultural exports in total agricultural world exports. 'Trade' is the share of total African exports in total world exports.

Many studies point out the low productivity of capital in Africa as compared to other developing regions. One ought to keep in mind the fact that problems arise in estimating the indicator. According to the World Bank (1989, p. 25), productivity of capital in Africa in 1980 was only a tenth part of productivity in South Asia. Furthermore, during the 1980s productivity of capital has decreased dramatically. However, national figures are not available so that an in-depth analysis cannot be performed.

As has already been mentioned, an increase in production can also be realised by increasing capital stock. For an increasing number of machines will enable labourers to increase labour productivity. The accumulation of capital stock is realised by positive net investment, in other words by a positive difference between gross investment and investment required to maintain the existing capital stock, that is capital replacement.

Table 2.6 shows that the value of investment in relation to GDP is smaller in Africa than in other developing countries. In particular in Madagascar and the Ivory Coast the investment share in GDP is very small. Tanzania is an exceptional case since investment here is relatively high. Also in Africa investment in relation to GDP has dropped during the 1980s. This drop was especially strong in the Ivory Coast, Kenya, and Nigeria. However, in Ghana and Tanzania the investment share in GDP rose.

Table 2.6 presents figures on gross investment since data on depreciation are not available. Some studies, however, show that net investment was even negative during the 1980s which triggered the destruction of capital. This is in sharp contrast with

Table 2.6 The share of investment in GDP

	INV/ GDP (1981)	PRINV/ GDP (1981)	PUINV/ GDP (1981)	INV/ GDP (1991)	PRINV/ GDP (1991)	PUINV/ GDP (1991)
Africa	22	12	10	16	10	05
East Asia	29	18	10	38	25	11
South Asia	24	11	09	22	12	10
Latin America	24	15	09	19	15	04
Ghana	07	04	03	16	08	08
Ivory Coast	24	11	11	08	04	04
Kenya	23	13	10	19	11	08
Madagascar	09	02	06	08	02	06
Nigeria	23	07	17	16	06	10
Tanzania	22	12	10	33	21	13

Sources: Miller and Sumlinski, 1994; World Bank, 1993b, Table 13

Notes: INV = total investment; PRINV = private investment; PUINV = public investment. Private and public investment together do not always equal total investment since PRINV and PUINV have been based on a subgroup of countries in various regions. The data on Ghana and Madagascar presented as data from 1981 actually refer to 1984.

developments during the 1970s. During this decade investment increased sharply which culminated in an investment rate of 23 per cent in 1976 (Elbadawi *et al.*, 1992, p. 11).

Total investment of a country consists of investment made by the private and the public sector. In Africa public investment as a percentage of GDP decreased strongly during the 1980s. Especially in Nigeria and the Ivory Coast this drop in public investment was substantial. In Ghana and Tanzania the percentage of public investment in GDP rose. The share of private investment in GDP also decreased. However, this decrease was not that large for Africa as a whole since private investment in Nigeria stayed fairly level. Nevertheless, the drop in private investment is still quite worrying.

2.4 The small volume of domestic savings

Investment is possible only if sufficient financial means are available. These means may derive from domestic and foreign savings (see Appendix 2). This section will centre around domestic savings. Foreign savings will be discussed in Sections 2.5 and 2.6.

At present, the share of domestic savings in the African GDP is very small in comparison to other developing regions (Table 2.7). Domestic savings dropped sharply during the 1980s after having increased during the 1970s. This is a rather striking phenomenon when compared to the situation in South Asia – a region about as poor as Africa. The decrease was especially substantial in Nigeria, Tanzania and the Ivory Coast. In Nigeria, however, a striking revolution of this tendency has taken place since 1989; in 1988 the share of domestic savings in GDP was no more than 15 per cent. In view of Nigeria's influence of the overall figure for Africa, for the other African countries the share of domestic savings in GDP is often smaller than the average mentioned in Table 2.7.

Table 2.7 The share of gross domestic savings in GDP

	1971	1980	1991
Africa	15	22	12
East Asia	26	31	38
South Asia	15	15	20
Latin America	19	23	22
Ghana	10	05	08
Ivory Coast	26	22	15
Kenya	17	18	19
Madagascar	05	−1	−1
Nigeria	16	32	23
Tanzania	22	10	−11

Source: World Bank, 1993b, Table 14

Domestic savings in a particular country per definition equal income minus total consumption (see Appendix 2). Since both the government – for example in the shape of the wages of civil servants – and the private sector are consumers, total domestic savings are influenced by both sectors. Therefore, it will be rather clarifying to consider the development of government consumption and the consumption by the private sector. For Africa the share of private (government) consumption in GDP increased from 66 (13) per cent in 1980 to 71 (17) per cent of GDP in 1991 (World Bank, 1989, Table 4; World Bank, 1993a, Table 9). Hence, the decreasing share of domestic savings in GDP in Africa is the result of both an increase in private and public consumption. What is rather remarkable is the sharp overall increase in government consumption for Africa, in particular in comparison to the other regions, where this increase was rather modest.

Adding up government investment expressed as a percentage of GDP (Table 2.6) and government consumption expressed as a percentage of GDP provides an indication of the degree to which the government monopolises the economy. Despite the decrease of investment, this monopoly appears to be significant. The fact that this is very much the result of the volume of public consumption is quite alarming. For economic growth is very much determined by the volume of investment by both the private and the public sector.

By solely considering public consumption or investment a judgement cannot be passed on the influence of the government on the economy and on the fact whether or not government expenditure is extravagant. The government also spends money in many different ways, not all of which are considered government consumption or investment, for example granting subsidies and paying interest. Furthermore, the government collects taxes which obviously affects the overall economy as well. Therefore, it is important to consider the difference between total government expenditure and government income – the government deficit. Moreover, total domestic private savings minus government deficit makes the volume of domestic savings available for financing private investment (see Appendix 2). In the case of the given private savings and foreign savings, therefore, a larger government deficit implies that the available means for private investment decrease.

Data on regional situations are not available, therefore I present data only on the six selected African countries. Table 2.8 shows that for 1991 in all countries government expenditure is considerably higher than government receipts, that is there are government deficits. Africa as a whole has a government budget deficit of about 10 per cent of GDP (United Nations, 1989, p. 100). Table 2.8 also shows that in Ghana government expenditure and receipts have grown steeply during the 1980s. In Madagascar on the other hand both government expenditure and government receipts have dropped dramatically during this period. Moreover, the share of the government deficit in GDP decreased. In the early 1980s Nigeria's government budget was positive but turned negative in the late 1980s. In Kenya, too, the budgetary position of the government deteriorated during the 1980s.

It is interesting to consider the structure of central government receipts. In Africa the basis for levying taxes is narrow. Large parts of the tax proceeds consist of value added tax (VAT) and excise (tax on food articles) and of taxes on international trade

Table 2.8 Expenditure and receipts of central government (percentage of GDP)

	Expend. 1970–75	Expend. 1980–85	Expend. 1991	Receipts 1970–75	Receipts 1980–85	Receipts 1991
Ghana	19.1	10.6	19.8	15.2	7.1	15.0
Ivory Coast	24.5	37.2	35.4	–	26.6	24.0
Kenya	20.0	25.9	30.5	17.3	20.9	22.1
Madagascar	15.4	27.9	15.9	14.0	13.7	9.4
Nigeria	10.8	12.7	23.2	13.6	17.8	20.3
Tanzania	24.7	28.5	26.3	18.9	19.9	18.3

Source: Foroutan, 1993, Table 5

transactions, such as import and export tariffs, and taxes on currency transactions. As part of international taxes, tariffs are especially important. In Africa as a whole the share of tariffs in total government revenue is between 25 and 30 per cent (United Nations, 1989, p. 113) which indicates the importance of tariff revenues to Africa. Due to the fact that many African countries are dependent of taxes on international transactions many of these countries have introduced such high trade tariffs (Nash, 1993, p. 4).

To some extent the various possibilities for financing the government budget deficit determine the degree to which a deficit is manageable. A government deficit may be financed in different ways. The government may cover her deficit by borrowing from the private sector (by means of issuing bonds on the capital market), by borrowing from the domestic banking sector (e.g. the central bank), or by borrowing money and receiving unilateral transfers from abroad.

In Africa capital markets are almost completely absent, which means that the government can only occasionally finance its deficit by issuing government bonds. Moreover, the private banking sector is underdeveloped so that deficits are mainly financed by borrowing from the central bank (monetary finance, i.e. creating money) and by borrowing money from abroad.

About 60 per cent of Africa's government deficit is financed by foreign loans (United Nations, 1989, p. 108); this does not include development aid. If this is included, the foreign share in the financing of government deficits will increase even more. The slight possibilities of increasing 'domestic' taxes and the absence of a well-developed capital market imply that an increase in government expenditure should be financed to a large extent by an increase in taxes on trade transactions, by increasing foreign financial means, or by increasing money creation. All three possibilities involve significant drawbacks. Increasing tax on trade transactions goes against all attempts of liberalising trade. An increase in development aid leads to an increase in foreign debt (that is, if these transfers are not donations) which may have negative effects. Moreover, Africa's access to foreign loans is severely supply constrained. Foreign countries themselves decide whether or not Africa is offered the possibility of borrowing money. An increase in monetary finance may involve increasing inflation. If foreign aid is not increased and if the disadvantages of other financing options for

Africa (particularly monetary finance and tariffs) are estimated only one possibility remains: a decrease in government expenditure. Naturally, the ultimate result depends to a large extent on the way in which the decrease in government expenditure is realised. A decrease in government expenditure by reducing salaries, by laying off civil servants, or by reducing subsidies will have entirely different political and economic effects than reducing expenditure for infrastructure.

2.5 Foreign capital flows: a decrease in real capital inflows

In the previous section it has been noted that domestic investment can be financed both by domestic and by foreign savings. Disregarding international changes in reserves, foreign savings consist of net capital inflows, that is gross capital inflow minus capital outflow, minus net interest payments to foreign countries. How did capital flows to Africa develop during the past decades? Table 2.9 provides an insight.

Foreign capital flows to Africa and other regions have increased sharply during the 1970s. Africa's nominal inflow has increased almost tenfold during this period. However, in the early 1980s total capital flows decreased strongly. Since 1986 financial flows to Africa have started to increase again. The same process can be observed in the six countries selected. The decrease in capital flows in the early 1980s was especially dramatic in the Ivory Coast and Nigeria. Nigeria and Kenya are the only countries where capital flows decreased further after 1986; at present net inflow in Nigeria is in fact negative.

These data are presented in nominal terms and therefore have not been corrected for inflation and fluctuations in the exchange rates. If these data were to be corrected

Table 2.9 Total net capital inflows (millions of US dollars)

	1970	1980	1986	1992
Africa	1644	15139	11218	17260
East Asia	2241	12819	12226	51647
South Asia	1388	6345	8604	10126
Latin America	4194	30159	11402	30796
Ghana	104	181	202	775
Ivory Coast	94	1138	133	628
Kenya	67	630	504	494
Madagascar	35	348	348	435
Nigeria	259	773	270	−342
Tanzania	60	848	674	1026

Source: World Bank, 1993c

Note: Data refer to long-term capital flows (debt increasing flows + direct investment + portfolio flows + donations), excluding technical cooperation and IMF means.

for these aspects, the real value of foreign capital flows to Africa since 1990 would appear to be decreasing strongly. In 1992 the volume of capital flows in real terms has more or less returned to the 1984 level (OECD, 1993, Table III.7). The capital inflows for Africa recalculated in real terms amount to US$14 billion in 1984, US$25 billion in 1989 and US$17 billion in 1992.[5]

Foreign capital flows consist of loans from and donations by multilateral institutions and authorities, direct investment, and loans from the private sector. Foreign capital flows to Africa mainly consist of flows from the first group, that is official capital flows. Private capital flows such as commercial bank loans and direct investment are of minor importance. Table 2.10 shows that Nigeria and the Ivory Coast – and to a smaller degree Ghana and Kenya, countries that managed occasionally to attract direct investment – were granted extensive loans from the private sector during the 1970s. However, these countries now have to rely on the official flows again. With reference to Africa the small share of private flows has decreased further during the 1980s. The 1970 share of official flows is actually very much influenced by occasional direct investment which took place in 1970. After correcting for this, the share increases to 73 per cent. Thus it appears that private flows have been of importance to Africa only for a short period of time – from the late 1970s until the early 1980s. The better part of these private flows was destined for Nigeria and the Ivory Coast as bank loans. The remarkably strong decrease in the share of private flows in Nigeria and the Ivory Coast in the early 1980s is a direct result of the fact that international bank loans to these countries came to an absolute halt.

Of the net capital flows the share of development aid particularly is rather large. With reference to Africa as a whole this share amounts to more than 90 per cent (OECD, 1993). The great significance of development aid is also validated by the

Table 2.10 Share of official capital flows (percentage of total capital flows)

	1970	1980	1986	1992
Africa	53	48	95	89
East Asia	70	31	44	17
South Asia	94	85	76	70
Latin America	24	18	76	11
Ghana	37	115	81	97
Ivory Coast	49	18	98	95
Kenya	51	52	79	103
Madagascar	74	68	97	96
Nigeria	27	10	144	−148
Tanzania	83	87	99	96

Source: World Bank, 1993c

Notes: Shares have been calculated by dividing the entries of Official Creditors (part of public and publicly guaranteed debts) plus Grants by Net Resource Flows. The result may be a share of over 100 per cent if net private capital flows are negative in a certain year.

comparison of the share of aid in GDP in several regions. In Africa this share amounts to an average 10 per cent whereas in East Asia and in Latin America it is just 1 per cent. This image is reinforced when one realises that the African average is very much determined by Nigeria, where the share of aid in GDP is a mere 0.8 per cent. In many other African countries the share of aid is above average – the extreme cases being Mozambique, Tanzania and Guinea Bissau. In these countries aid expressed as a percentage of GDP amounted to 69, 34 and 43 per cent respectively in 1991 (World Bank, 1994b, Table 19).

As a conclusion to this section, I point to the recent phenomenon of African capital flight. This flow of financial means from Africa to foreign countries appears to be quite sizeable and is therefore a point of particular interest in discussing Africa. There are no reliable data on capital flight since it is an illegal activity. Estimates do exist, but these differ strongly from each other and are dependent on the method chosen.[6] Therefore, a presentation of the World Bank calculations for Africa as a whole (World Bank, 1993c, p. 13) will suffice. The World Bank estimates the current total volume of capital flight in Africa to be at least 90 per cent of GDP.

2.6 Debt crisis: extensive debt obligations

The net foreign financial means available for investment in a particular country are also determined by the volume of interest payments on foreign debt; this leads us to the debt crisis. The most important developments in this field will be discussed briefly.[7]

In the early 1970s Africa's foreign debt was limited (in 1970 less than US$6 billion: World Bank, 1993c). Later, African debt increased dramatically especially during the 1970s. In 1992 African debt was about US$194 billion (World Bank, 1993c). Total debt in Africa is high but not excessive in comparison to the other regions. Most highly indebted countries are Latin American: the collective debt of Brazil and Mexico – over US$200 billion – exceeds Africa's total debt.

The preceding observations do not imply that Africa's burden of debt is rather slight. In order to be able to pass a judgement on this matter it is necessary to consider several ratios. Table 2.11 presents the development of debt in relation to GNP and the debt service (amortisation plus interest) in relation to exports, i.e. debt service ratio. Compared to the other regions Africa has a high debt in relation to GNP. In order to judge the real annual burden we should consider the debt service ratio. This ratio indicates the share of export proceeds that is used for meeting debt obligations. The debt/GNP ratio is less relevant since it does not really indicate the amount actually paid. This ratio would be more relevant in the long term since it does – to a certain extent – compare the volume of the debt to the volume of net assets, in this context expressed by GNP. Since a large part of the debt is unlikely to be repaid, this ratio loses in significance.

During the 1980s Africa's debt service ratio shows a cyclic development: first it increased strongly, later the ratio decreased again. In 1992 the ratio was

Table 2.11 Debt ratios (percentage)

	FD/GNP 1980	FD/GNP 1986	FD/GNP 1992	DS/E 1980	DS/E 1986	DS/E 1992
Africa	30.1	63.5	69.7	9.7	24.9	16.9
East Asia	18.3	33.7	29.7	13.6	24.3	12.9
South Asia	17.5	28.4	36.9	11.9	29.3	20.7
Latin America	37.2	66.7	41.7	37.1	43.7	29.8
Ghana	31.8	48.8	63.1	13.1	28.4	26.7
Ivory Coast	76.9	127.7	207.1	38.7	35.1	31.5
Kenya	48.2	65.6	75.9	21.0	34.9	24.5
Madagascar	30.6	106.4	153.9	17.1	47.9	20.7
Nigeria	10.1	60.5	110.7	4.2	32.7	30.6
Tanzania	48.3	89.8	268.4	19.6	29.2	32.5

Source: World Bank, 1993c

Notes: FD/GNP = total foreign debt divided by GNP; DS/E = debt service instalments plus interest payments divided by exports.

approximately 17 per cent, which implies that 17 per cent of the proceeds from exports flow back abroad as interest payments and amortisations. Unlike in East Asia, the recent decrease of the debt service ratio is the result of a freeze or a postponement of payments on debt rather than an increase in exports or of a decrease in interest and amortisation *obligations*. Moreover, in recent years the increase in debt is the result of accumulated debt obligations (i.e. arrears) rather than of contracting new loans. Many African countries have decided not to fulfil their obligations, simply because they were unable to or because they did not really fear the negative results of their actions. Indeed, it is not really expected that Africa will be able to borrow from private banks in future, so little importance is attached to threats by banks not to put new loans at Africa's disposal. In 1991 only half of the debt obligations was fulfilled (Husain, 1993, p. 22).

The structure of Africa's debt differs from the Latin American and East Asian debts to a significant extent. Latin America and East Asia have debts with private banks mainly, whereas Africa's main debts are with governments and multilateral institutions (Table 2.12). This is not surprising taking into account the structure of capital flows to Africa. The large volume of debts with governments and multilateral institutions resulted in Africa – to a much greater extent than, for example, Latin America – in borrowing on concessionary terms (particularly, low interest rates). The share of concessionary debt in Africa's total debt was over 25 per cent in 1991. For the Low Income Countries it even amounted to 60 per cent (Husain, 1993, Table V).

As we have seen, net available foreign means are determined by net foreign capital flows and obligations concerning interest. If this fact is taken into account, the net foreign capital flow to Africa decreases about US$10 billion in 1992 (World Bank, 1993c). The net foreign capital inflow is still positive but much smaller than it appeared to be in the previous section.

Table 2.12 Share of official debts in total long-term debt

	1970	1980	1986	1992
Africa	71	44	63	75
East Asia	64	57	50	59
South Asia	94	91	78	78
Latin America	52	31	41	44
Ghana	65	89	85	93
Ivory Coast	56	29	51	75
Kenya	74	58	85	82
Madagascar	96	64	85	93
Nigeria	79	23	45	65
Tanzania	97	87	92	96

Source: World Bank, 1993c

Note: The shares refer to government and government guaranteed debt.

2.7 Summary

Africa is characterised by a crisis in the agricultural and the industrial sector. In both sectors growth decreased or even came to a halt in the 1970s and 1980s. Especially the crisis in the agricultural sector had far-reaching effects. In most African countries the agricultural sector is a very important sector. Moreover, the export of some agricultural products make up the main constituent of the export proceeds of many African countries. The agricultural crisis manifests itself in Africa's decreasing market share on world markets.

In comparison with other developing regions, in Africa efficiency and volume of investment are low and domestic savings are small. With respect to foreign capital flows it is noticeable that Africa is now almost completely dependent on development aid. Private commercial capital flows have always been of minor importance to Africa, but during the 1980s these flows dropped even further. Total nominal capital flows to Africa increased in the late 1980s. However, expressed in constant prices there seems to be a decreasing total inflow of foreign means in recent years. The large share of official capital flows manifests itself in the structure of Africa's foreign debt. To most countries this debt consists mainly of debts to governments and multilateral institutions. Nigeria and the Ivory Coast are among the few African countries that used to qualify for international bank loans. Africa's burden of debt is great. Yet, this observation should be further explained. Since many countries have decided not to fulfil their debt obligations and since the conditions attached to African debt are much more favourable (low interest rates, etc.), Africa's debt service/export ratio does not differ from that in the other developing regions. Of course, this does not imply that individual countries do not have any problems.

In the early 1990s several slight improvements seem to be setting in. For example, in a number of countries an increase in export growth and growth in GDP can be observed. However, it is premature to attach conclusions to this fact. Besides, the improvements are merely marginal. Africa is still in the middle of an economic crisis. This is not a recent phenomenon but rather one that was started as early as the early 1970s.

Appendix 1 to Chapter 2: Some basic indicators

This appendix presents some basic indicators for the African countries; it does not attempt to give a complete overview of economic and social indicators. The figures presented serve only to highlight some of the differences between the countries in Africa. Differences with respect to the size and the population density are reflected by the figures on the area, and the size and growth of the population; differences with respect to the current economic and social situation are reflected by GNP per capita and the Human Development Index; differences with respect to economic development in the 1980s are reflected by the growth rates with respect to GNP and inflation. The Development Reports and the World Tables of the World Bank and the Human Development Reports of the UN give more detailed descriptions.

The data are self-explaining so do not need further explanation; only the indicator 'human development index' warrants some discussion. Traditionally, figures for GNP (or GDP) per capita serve as indicators for the degree of development of a country. However, it can be criticised along several lines. GNP (GDP) figures, in general, do not take into account informal production, which is substantial in most African countries. An increase in GNP, therefore, may give the wrong suggestion that total production is increased: it may simply be the result of a shift from informal production to formal production, without an increase in overall production. However, since well-developed indicators taking informal production into account do not exist GNP still remains the best indicator as far as the measurement of production is concerned. Moreover, the GNP indicator may be criticised due to its narrow scope. GNP per capita does not take into account all kinds of social events, such as income distribution, so that the use of this indicator may not give a correct picture of the 'development' of a country. Therefore, the UN have recently started to calculate Human Development Indices as a substitute for GNP per capita as development indicator. The Human Development Index is meant to be a better socio-economic measure of a country than GNP per capita. Although the construction of the Human Development Index has been refined and corrected several times since its introduction, the basic construction method remained. The measure is a composite of three basic components of human development: longevity, measured by life expectancy; knowledge, measured by a combination of adult literacy and mean years of schooling; and standard of living, measured by the real GDP per capita adjusted for local cost of living (UN, 1994, p. 91). A higher figure corresponds with a better socio-economic development.

Table A2.1 Some basic indicators

	Area (thousand sq. km)	Inflation 1980–92	per capita GNP (growth: 1980–92)	per capita GNP (US dollars 1992)	Human development index (1992)	Population (millions; 1992)	Population (growth: 1980–92)
Benin	113	1.7	−0.7	410	0.261	5.0	3.1
Botswana	582	12.6	6.1	2790	0.670	1.4	3.4
Burkina Faso	274	3.5	1.0	300	0.203	9.5	2.6
Burundi	28	4.5	1.3	210	0.276	5.8	2.8
Cameroon	475	3.5	−1.5	820	0.447	12.2	2.8
Cape Verde	4	9.3	3.0	850	0.474	0.4	—
Cent. Afric. Rep.	623	4.6	−1.5	410	0.249	3.2	2.6
Chad	1284	0.9	3.4	220	0.212	6.0	2.4
Comoros	2	5.6	−1.3	510	0.331	0.5	—
Congo	342	0.5	−0.8	1030	0.461	2.4	3.1
Eq. Guinea	28	—	—	330	0.276	0.4	—
Ethiopia	1222	2.8	−1.9	110	0.249	54.8	3.1
Gabon	268	2.3	−3.7	4450	0.525	1.2	3.4
Gambia	11	17.8	−0.4	370	0.215	1.0	—
Ghana	239	38.7	−0.1	450	0.382	15.8	3.2
Guinea	246	—	—	510	0.191	6.1	2.6
Guinea-Bissau	36	59.3	1.6	220	0.224	1.0	1.9
Ivory Coast	322	1.9	−4.7	670	0.370	12.9	3.8
Kenya	580	9.3	0.2	310	0.434	25.7	3.6
Lesotho	30	13.2	−0.5	590	0.476	1.9	2.7
Madagascar	587	16.4	−2.4	230	0.396	12.4	2.9
Malawi	118	15.1	−0.1	210	0.260	9.1	3.2

Table A2.1 *(Continued)*

	Area (thousand sq. km)	Inflation 1980–92	per capita GNP (growth: 1980–92)	per capita GNP (US dollars 1992)	Human development index (1992)	Population (millions; 1992)	Population (growth: 1980–92)
Mali	1240	3.7	−2.7	310	0.214	9.0	2.6
Mauritania	1026	8.3	−0.8	530	0.254	2.1	2.4
Mauritius	2	8.6	5.6	2700	0.778	1.1	1.1
Mozambique	802	38.0	−3.6	60	0.252	16.5	2.6
Namibia	824	12.3	−1.0	1610	0.425	1.5	3.0
Niger	1267	1.7	−4.3	280	0.209	8.2	3.3
Nigeria	924	19.4	−0.4	320	0.348	101.9	3.0
Rwanda	26	3.6	−0.6	250	0.274	7.3	2.9
Senegal	197	5.2	0.1	780	0.322	7.8	2.9
Seychelles	0.28	3.3	3.2	5460	0.685	0.069	—
Sierra Leone	72	60.8	−1.4	160	0.209	4.4	2.4
Somalia	638	49.7	—	—	0.217	8.3	3.1
Sudan	2506	42.8	—	—	0.276	26.5	2.7
Swaziland	17	11.8	1.6	1090	0.513	0.9	—
Tanzania	945	25.3	0.0	110	0.306	25.9	3.0
Togo	57	4.2	−1.8	390	0.311	3.9	3.3
Uganda	236	—	—	170	0.272	17.5	2.6
Zaïre	2345	—	−1.8	469	0.341	39.8	—
Zambia	753	48.4	—	1010	0.352	8.3	3.2
Zimbabwe	391	14.4	−0.9	570	0.474	10.4	3.3
Africa	24274	15.6	−0.8	530	0.395	543.0	3.0

Sources: Most figures are from World Bank, 1994b. GNP per capita figures for Zaïre and Zambia refer to 1991 and are taken from UN 1994, Table 2.

A comparison of the figures for GNP per capita and the Human Development Index shows that there exist considerable differences between the ranking of the countries using both indicators. Kenya, Madagascar, Tanzania, Burundi and Mozambique belong to the very low developed countries in the case where the GNP per capita indicator is used, whereas their picture seems to be much better when the Human Development Index is used. Otherwise, the Central African Republic, Gambia, Burkina Faso and Guinea are relatively poorly developed in the case where the Human Development Index is used, whereas the GNP per capita indicator gives a much more positive picture for these countries.

Although I find the development of the UN index promising and although I agree with the view that development cannot be associated only with an increase in GNP per capita, this book will mainly use GNP figures and other traditional economic indicators for highlighting economic developments. The basic reason is that it is not yet possible to make comparisons across countries over time by using a Human Development Index, since the estimation of this index has been started very recently and since the construction of the index has changed continuously. However, in Chapter 8 I shall use 'social' indicators to highlight effects of the adjustment programmes on social development.

Appendix 2 to Chapter 2: Macroeconomic identities

In this second appendix several basic macroeconomic identities will be discussed. In describing the macroeconomic situation in Africa I used these macroeconomic identities several times. Furthermore, in the following chapters I shall use some of the identities that are derived in this appendix. Readers who are not interested in the derivation of these identities will have no difficulty understanding the contents of this book without consulting this appendix.

Table A2.2 presents the non-financial transactions in a simple economy between firms, households, the government, the rest of the world (ROW) and the banking system. I abstract from interest payments between sectors, from transfers, from indirect taxes and subsidies, and from profits by public enterprises.[8] The rows indicate the way the income is obtained, the columns indicate what this money is spent on. The total of the rows levels the total of the columns.

Firms

The second row indicates the fact that a firm earns its income by means of selling investment goods to other firms (I_p), investment goods to the government (I_g), consumer goods to households and to the government (C_p and C_g), and exports to foreign countries (X). In a mathematical equation total production of firms (Q) is:

A1 $Q = C_p + I_p + C_g + I_g + X$

From the second column it can be seen that part of the production by firms is intended for firms (I_g). Thus investments by firms are both expenditure and receipts of firms. For convenience it is assumed that only firms import goods from abroad and that all imports are intermediate goods. Firms manufacture these imports (Z) into end products, and then these are sold to the government, foreign countries and households. Income, which in this case equals GDP, per definition equals the total production of firms minus imports:

A2 $\text{GDP} = Q - Z = C_p + I_p + C_g + I_g + X - Z$

Firms channel the income (GDP) to households as a compensation for services rendered, such as labour. The difference between the receipts and expenditure of firms is investment which is financed with loans on the financial market.

Households

Households receive the income which they will spend on consumer goods, taxes (T) and savings (S). Savings are described here as that part of the disposable income ($Q - Z - T = \text{GDP} - T$) that is not used in consumption (this is the regular description of the term 'savings'). From the column households it follows that:

A3 $\quad Q - Z = \text{GDP} = C_p + T + S_p$

If equation A2 equates with equation A3, I arrive at the following identity:

A4 $\quad (S_p - I) + (T - C_g) = (X - Z)$

The variable I denotes total investment (private and public investment). Equation A4 shows that the trade balance ($X - Z$) per definition equals the difference between private savings and investment plus taxes minus consumer expenditure by the government. This equation proves that the situation with respect to the trade balance can improve only if private savings or taxes increase or if investment or government consumption decrease. As can be inferred from the table, equation A4 can also be found by adding up the row that refers to the financial market. This row indicates the surplus or deficit of the various sectors. The surpluses of a particular sector are channelled to the deficits of another sector through the financial market. In the equilibrium the deficit of one sector is always financed by the surplus of another sector.

Equation A4 may also be represented differently. The difference between taxes and government consumption ($T - C_g$) is often called government savings (S_g). Moreover, the deficit on the trade balance ($Z - X$) is regarded as foreign savings (S_f). Taking the above into account, equation A4 is presented as follows:

A4a $\quad I = I_p + I_g = S_p + S_g + S_f = S_d + S_f$

where S_d denotes total domestic savings. Equation A4a shows that domestic investment is financed by domestic savings (by households and the government) and by foreign savings.

Government

The government levies taxes which are paid by households, and the government buys goods from firms. The difference between the two is the government deficit ($C_g + I_g - T$). A government deficit may be financed by loans on the financial market.

With the help of equations A4 and A4a it can be inferred that private investment equals private savings minus the government deficit plus foreign savings:

A4b $\quad I_p = S_p - I_g - C_g + T + S_f$

Rest of the world

Foreign countries (ROW) buy goods from and sell goods to the homeland. The difference is the trade balance surplus or deficit of the homeland.

Banking system

It is presupposed that the banking system fulfils an intermediary function only. The banking system channels savings from one sector to another. The banking system therefore has no independent receipts and expenditure; that is why the column with relation to the banking system is empty.

Next I shall discuss the ways the different sectors finance their deficits and how the surpluses of other sectors are used. Table A2.3 present an overview. The second row is identical to the penultimate row in Table A2.2. In Table A2.3 I have not distinguished between households and firms for the sake of convenience. These sectors have been combined to make up one sector, the private sector.

Private sector (households and firms)

I have assumed that the private sector can obtain credit from the domestic banking system (the domestic credit market: ΔDC_p) and from the foreign countries (the foreign credit market: ΔFC_p). The total amount of financial means (savings plus credit) can be used to finance investment. The positive difference between savings and credit on the one hand and investment on the other hand is held in the shape of money (ΔM):

A5 $S_p + \Delta DC_p + \Delta FC_p = I_p + \Delta M$

Government

The government in my simple economy can finance its deficit by means of loans from the domestic (ΔDC_g) and the foreign banking system (ΔFC_g). From the government column it can be inferred that the government finances consumption plus investment

Table A2.2 Non-financial transactions between sectors

	Firms	Households	Government	ROW	Banking	Total
Firms	I_p	C_p	C_g+I_g	X		Q
Households	$Q-Z$					$Q-Z$
Government		T				T
ROW	Z					Z
Financial market	$-I_p$	S_p	$T-C_g-I_g$	$Z-X$	0	0
Total	Q	$Q-Z$	T	Z	0	

expenditures by levying taxes and by borrowing from the domestic and the foreign banking system:

$$A6 \quad T + \Delta DC_g + \Delta FC_g = I_g + C_g$$

Rest of the world

From the fourth column in Table A2.3 I can infer that a deficit in the trade balance per definition equals the inflow of foreign financial means minus the decrease in international reserves (ΔRES):

$$A7 \quad Z - X = \Delta FC_g + \Delta FC_p - \Delta RES = \Delta FC - \Delta RES$$

where ΔF denotes total capital inflow. Equation A7 reflects the balance of payments of the homeland. A balance of payments presents all foreign transactions of a particular country. The equation concerning the balance of payments indicates the way a country finances the deficit in its trade balance, or the way in which a country uses a surplus in the trade balance. When a particular country has a deficit in the trade balance (imports exceeding exports) this may be financed by obtaining foreign credit (an increase in foreign capital flows). When the inflow of foreign capital is insufficient to finance the deficit in the trade balance, a decrease in foreign reserves will be the result.[9] Thus, a deficit in the trade balance per definition equals the foreign capital inflow plus the decrease in the supply of international reserves.

In many macroeconomic studies the equation A7 is rewritten somewhat by considering changes in the international reserves as part of foreign credit. The following equation results from this rewriting:

$$A7a \quad Z - X = \Delta FC_a$$

in this context $\Delta FC_a = \Delta FC - \Delta RES$.

Considering the fact that the deficit in the trade balance per definition equals total domestic investment minus total domestic savings, equation A7a can be rewritten as

$$A7b \quad I - S_d = \Delta FC_a$$

Equation A7b shows that domestic investment can be financed by domestic savings and by foreign capital inflows.

The banking system

The banking system in my simple economy comprises a central bank and a commercial bank. For the sake of convenience these two banks have been combined into one single bank. The banking system intervenes in the international currency market, that is international currencies are bought and sold. Buying foreign currency results in an increase of the supply of international reserves (ΔRES). Since international reserves are bought with the domestic currency, this purchase will lead to an increase in the domestic money supply (ΔM). Moreover, the banking system grants loans to the government and to the private sector ($\Delta DC_p + \Delta DC_g$).

The obligations of the banking system consist of money held by households. For a historical reason, money held by households is considered an obligation to the central bank. In earlier days one could go to the central bank and exchange money for gold. Claims by the banking system consist of loans to the government and the private sector plus the international reserves. The international reserves are the claims by the homeland's central bank since the international reserves are held in foreign currencies; thus this central bank actually has a claim on the foreign central bank. Again it used to be possible to go abroad and exchange foreign reserves against gold. Studying the banking system column the following equation can be deduced:

A8 $\Delta M = \Delta RES + \Delta DC_g + \Delta DC_p = \Delta RES + \Delta DC$

where ΔDC denotes total domestic credit.

Equation A8 shows that the money supply in a country increases if international reserves increase or if the government or the private sector are granted loans by the banking system.

Table A2.3 Financial transactions

	Private sector	Government	ROW	Banking	Total
Surplus	$-I_p+S_p$	$T-C_g-I_g$	$Z-X$	0	0
Dom. cred.	ΔDC_p	ΔDC_g		$-\Delta DC_p-\Delta DC_g$	0
Foreign cred.	ΔFC_p	ΔFC_g	$-\Delta FC_p-\Delta FC_g+\Delta RES$	$-\Delta RES$	0
Fin. market	$-\Delta M$			$+\Delta M$	0
Total	0	0	0	0	0

Note: Dom. cred. and Foreign cred. refer to the domestic and the foreign credit markets.

Notes

1 The LLDCs are a group of developing countries classified by the United Nations on the basis of their per capita income, the share of intermediate goods in production, and the degree of education.

2 GDP is the total final output of goods and services domestically produced by residents and non-residents. GNP is the income received for productive activity by domestic residents. The difference between the two mainly arises from net factor payments from abroad (i.e. interest payments and labour income accruing to domestic residents from abroad).

3 South Asia comprises Bangladesh, Bhutan, India, Nepal, Pakistan and Sri Lanka. East Asia refers to China, Fiji, Indonesia, Korea, Laos, Malaysia, Mongolia, Papua New Guinea, the Philippines, Samoa, the Solomon Islands, Thailand and Vanuata. Latin America consists of all countries in Latin America and the Caribbean.

4 From 1988 to 1992 the average growth rate of GDP in Africa was about 2.7 per cent. This is an improvement compared to the previous period but it is still lower than the average population growth.

5 For the sake of completeness it should be mentioned that the OECD definition of foreign capital flows differs from the World Bank definition. Furthermore, I refer to the observation made in the introduction to this chapter. Data from different sources do rather differ. This is especially the case with capital flows. Readers therefore should not wonder at the fact that the considerable drop in the real value of capital flows is not that extreme in some other sources.

6 I refer to Hermes and Lensink (1992) for a discussion of the methods used for calculating the volume of capital flight, and for calculations for several African countries.

7 I refer to Abbott (1993) and Hermes (1992) for complete surveys well worth reading.

8 See Mills and Nallari (1992) for a derivation of macroeconomic identities that do take these aspects into account.

9 In this particular context I have neglected interest payments and transfers (development aid).

3 The causes of the crisis

The previous chapter has shown that Africa has to contend with an economic crisis which started as early as the early 1970s. The African crisis can be explained on the basis of two entirely different points of view. In correspondence with the distinction made in Chapter 1, the viewpoints of the neoliberal economists (Section 3.1) and the structuralists (Section 3.2) will be considered. This strict distinction between these schools of thought is not so very distinct in actual practice since most authors use both neoliberal and structuralist arguments.[1] The theoretical description of the causes of the crisis is followed by an overview of several empirical studies of the subject (Section 3.3). Section 3.4 concludes this chapter with a summary.

3.1 The causes of the crisis according to the neoliberals

According to the neoliberals the cause of the crisis is – to a large extent – the government policies pursued. The basic principle of their analysis is their faith in the market mechanism: the beneficial effects of market incentives, and the economically rational behaviour of individuals. They also stress the fact that a policy directed towards stimulating exports offers many advantages in comparison to a policy of import substitution. It is argued that an import substitution policy leads to inefficient production since enterprises are not stimulated to increase their efficiency due to a lack of competition.

The neoclassical trade theory and the vent for surplus theory

Because of the significance of trade to the neoliberal viewpoint, before entering into the causes of the African crisis, two theories showing the advantages of trade will be discussed: the neoclassical trade theory and the vent for surplus theory. The neoliberals base their analysis mainly on the neoclassical trade theory. I shall discuss the simplest version of the neoclassical trade theory, Ricardo's trade theory, which argues that each country will profit if they specialise in goods that offer them a comparative advantage. This can be illustrated with a simple example. I shall use two countries, for example, Ghana and Kenya, two products, cocoa and coffee, one production factor, labour, and assume full employment. I shall presuppose that in an autarky – before trade – Kenya produces ten kilo of cocoa or ten kilo of coffee per hour and that in an autarky Ghana can produce nine kilo of cocoa or three kilo of coffee an hour. Table 3.1 presents the autarky situation.

From Table 3.1 it can be concluded that Kenya can produce both more cocoa and more coffee per hour than Ghana. Ricardo shows that in this particular case it is mutually advantageous to trade both to Kenya and to Ghana. In order to understand this the term of alternative costs is introduced. Alternative costs are described as the number of articles a country will produce less if one extra article of the alternative good is produced. Using the data from Table 3.1, Table 3.2 presents the alternative costs to Kenya and Ghana.

Table 3.2 shows that the alternative costs of Kenya producing one extra kilo of cocoa equals one kilo of coffee. In other words, the production of one extra kilo of cocoa in Kenya can be realised only if it produces one kilo of coffee less; the extra cocoa has to be produced by a labourer who used to produce coffee. Obviously, the condition of full employment is crucial. In Kenya the alternative cost of producing one extra kilo of cocoa is one kilo of coffee. In Ghana the alternative cost of producing one extra kilo of cocoa is one-third kilo of coffee, and the alternative costs of producing one kilo of coffee are three kilo of cocoa.

On the basis of the alternative costs table, one can determine the article in which these countries have a comparative advantage. To have a comparative advantage in a particular article means that the alternative costs of producing this article are lower in one country than in another. Thus Kenya has a comparative advantage in producing coffee and Ghana has a comparative advantage in producing cocoa: extra production of coffee in Kenya is paid for with a smaller decrease in the production of cocoa than the extra production of coffee in Ghana is. Furthermore, the costs – expressed in coffee – of extra cocoa production are smaller in Ghana than in Kenya.

Ricardo's theory states that total production increases if each country specialises in the product in which it has a comparative advantage. In this particular case this means

Table 3.1 Production per hour

	Cocoa	Coffee
Kenya	10	10
Ghana	9	3

Table 3.2 Alternative costs

	Cocoa	Coffee
Kenya	1 pear	1 apple
Ghana	$\frac{1}{3}$ pears	3 apples

that Kenya should specialise in producing coffee and Ghana in the production of cocoa. Table 3.3 presents the results of the first step towards specialisation. This table shows the effects of an increase in production of one kilo of the product this country has a comparative advantage in.

Table 3.3 shows that the extra production of one kilo of coffee in Kenya involves a decrease in the cocoa production of one kilo of cocoa. In Ghana an increase in the cocoa production of one kilo leads to a decrease in the coffee production of one-third kilo. It also appears that the total production of cocoa has not changed and that the production of coffee has increased by two-thirds kilo. Next, Ricardo argues that the increase in the world production will be divided among the two countries due to trade. From his point of view Kenya ought to export coffee to Ghana in exchange for cocoa, and Ghana ought to export cocoa to Kenya in exchange for coffee. The price established on the world market – in this case the amount of coffee exchanged for cocoa – will be as follows: for exporting one kilo of coffee, Kenya receives more than one kilo of cocoa from Ghana, and for one exported kilo of cocoa to Kenya Ghana receives more than one-third kilo of coffee. Thus to both countries the total of goods available will increase. Both countries profit from the new situation because they specialise in the product in which they have a comparative advantage and because they start trading.

The neoclassical trade theory assumes that production factors are fully employed, that there is no unemployment. Clearly, for many developing countries this is not realistic. Probably, the vent for surplus theory, which is based on the assumption of unemployed resources in the autarky situation, gives a more realistic reason why developing countries may gain from trade. This theory states that trade enables countries to bring otherwise unemployed resources into employment. Trade, by extending the market on which products can be sold, may lead to a use of production factors which are otherwise wasted. So, the gains from trade according to the neoclassical trade theory stem from a better allocation of the fully employed production factors, whereas the gains from trade according to the vent for surplus theory are the result of a decrease in the amount of production factors unemployed. In other words, the vent for surplus theory states that trade enables a country to move from a point inside the production-possibility frontier, that is the curve showing the different combinations of outputs a country can produce, assuming a given technology and assuming that all production factors are fully employed, to a point on this frontier.

After this excursion I shall continue discussing the causes of the crisis according to the neoliberals. As has already been observed, they mainly consider the government

Table 3.3 Effects of specialisation

	Cocoa	Coffee
Kenya	−1	+1
Ghana	+1	$-\frac{1}{3}$
Total	0	$+\frac{2}{3}$

policy pursued in order to determine the causes of the crisis. The negative role of the government manifests itself in a number of activities, such as public enterprises, regulating distribution, regulating trade, and the agricultural cooperatives. The government has created an immense network of administrative and bureaucratic measures for the regulation of the economy. On the basis of their theory neoliberal economists are able to explain many of the stylised facts mentioned in Chapter 2.

The crisis in the agricultural and industrial sector and a decrease in the share of export

Neoliberal economists pay a great deal of attention to the crisis in the agricultural sector. They point out the great significance of the agricultural sector to Africa. A flourishing agricultural sector not only is of importance to a decrease in poverty in the country, but also contributes to the increasing productivity of the industrial sector. Szirmai (1994, Ch. 8) distinguishes the following possible contributions from the agricultural sector to the process of economic development:

1 In the early stages of economic development, part of the profits from a flourishing agricultural sector can be used for financing investment in the industrial sector.
2 The agricultural sector needs to produce a surplus of food so that food prices will remain low in urban sectors.
3 Exporting agricultural products is necessary for obtaining foreign currency which can be used abroad for buying machinery.
4 The agricultural sector supplies primary inputs such as food, wood and fibres to the industries.
5 The agricultural sector is a significant market for industrial products.
6 In the early stages of economic development the agricultural sector should supply labour to the industrial sector.

Contrary to the popular idea of the 1970s (see Chapter 1), the neoliberal economists contest the notion that the agricultural sector can be simply exploited for the benefit of the industrial sector. This attitude implies that there are costs involved in withdrawing labourers from the agricultural sector and on transferring agricultural profits to the industrial sector. Only if the agricultural sector is sufficiently stimulated by means of price incentives, transferring labourers from the agricultural sector will not be at the expense of agricultural production.

Neoliberal economists feel that the government very much hampered agricultural development by pursuing a faulty policy, First, the policy of 'cheap food' for the urban population results in low agricultural prices and damages to domestic food producers. In the long term this policy even leads to higher food prices due to a decrease in agricultural production. Second, inefficient marketing organisations, directed by the authorities, contribute to the fact that farmers receive lower prices for their products. In many African countries the government intervenes in the food market by means of marketing organisations aimed at guaranteeing the food supply. These organisations buy the products from the producers and sell them to the consumers. Most often, producer and consumer prices are set by the authorities. Third, there are high taxes on agricultural exports. Fourth, high tariffs and numerous import quotas force up the prices of imports necessary for the agricultural sector. The domestic industrial sector benefits from this policy which results in deteriorating internal terms of trade (prices of agricultural products in relation to the prices of industrial products). According to neoliberal economists these trade barriers are very much the cause of the decreasing market shares in the world market. Finally, there are overvalued currencies: the neoliberals often mention the negative effects of the overvalued real exchange rate.[2] Overvalued currencies stimulate the production for the domestic market whereas they hamper production for the world market. Since the agricultural sector is the traditional export sector, it is the sector damaged most by overvalued currencies. Overvalued currencies not only affect negatively exports, but also promote capital flight from Africa. If a currency is overvalued, devaluation is expected for the near future. In order to anticipate the possible devaluation of domestic capital, the money will be put out abroad. Moreover, neoliberal economists pay a great deal of attention to the causes of the real appreciation of currencies. Special attention is paid to the negative effects of the expansionary monetary and financial government policies. This expansionary policy will lead to an increase in the domestic money supply which will cause an increase in inflation resulting in domestic products becoming too expensive to be able to compete with foreign goods. The extensive inflow of development aid also contributes to the deterioration of export conditions of many African countries. It is felt that the great inflow of financial aid promotes the demand for non-tradable goods. The prices of goods produced for the world market will hardly be affected because these prices are established mainly on the actual world market. Thus, the extensive financial aid flows stimulate domestic producers to increase production for the domestic market at the expense of production for the world market.

The crisis in the industrial sector is closely related to the crisis in the agricultural sector, according to the neoliberal economists. As has already been explained, a thriving agricultural sector is vital to growth in the industrial sector. Furthermore, neoliberal economists point out the negative effects of sustained protection of the industrial sector. The policy of import substitution has led to the existence of inefficient companies that are unable to survive without any protection.

The low volume and efficiency of investment

According to the neoliberal economists, efficiency of investment is hindered by frequent price monitoring. Free market forces are not allowed to develop. Non-viable investment projects are carried out whereas all sorts of profitable investment projects are hampered. Moreover, the large number of inefficient government investments also contributes to the low average efficiency of investment. To a certain extent the low volume of investment is caused by the same problem: disruption of the market mechanism of prices which paralyses market incentives. Another important cause of the low volume of investment is the small volume of domestic savings. This leads to the absence of the required resources for investment.

The small volume of domestic savings

According to the neoliberal economists, the small volume of domestic savings has been caused mainly by the high government expenditure for consumption. This naturally leads to a decrease in domestic savings. An allied issue is the government deficit. Domestic savings that are available for private investment equal private savings plus the balance in the government budget (see Chapter 2). Thus, an increase in the government deficit per definition leads to a decrease in domestic savings available for private investment.

Domestic savings are also influenced negatively by the financial market policies pursued by African authorities. The interest policy in particular affects the situation in a negative manner. In most African countries, interest on savings and investment is kept artificially low aiming at promoting investment. According to the neoliberal economists this is counterproductive: low interest rates discourage domestic private savings which will result in a decrease in the amount of funds available for financing investment and thus in a decrease in investment.

A decrease in the real foreign capital inflow

Neoliberal economists feel that Africa's import substitution policy has been very important to the small and decreasing volume of the private capital flow to Africa. Many foreign investors are increasingly active on world markets. Investing in Africa, where there are many trade barriers, is not the logical thing to do. In this context, attention is also paid to the adverse effects of overvalued currencies. It is explicitly argued that foreign private capital flows to Africa will not increase in volume as long as profitability of investment is low.

Extensive debt service

The sources of the debt crisis, too, lie mainly in the policy pursued by the African authorities. In this context the neoliberals refer to the policy with respect to borrowing. The loans that were negotiated during the 1970s were not used productively, according to the neoliberal economists. A large part is said to have been used for keeping up consumption so that a positive contribution to economic growth was not made. Furthermore, the neoliberals refer to trade policy. Because in many African countries import substitution policies were pursued, these countries are now said to be less capable of flexibly anticipating external developments. This may seem odd since a country with an outward-oriented policy is indeed more sensitive to external developments. Still, this argument is plausible enough because a sudden deficit in foreign financial means – caused either by a freeze of loans or by a rapidly increasing volume of debt service – does not actually become a problem until this country proves to be absolutely unable to attract the required foreign currency. Africa was unable to attract foreign currency because its policy was inward-oriented, whereas East Asia proved to be much more capable of increasing its market share on the world market in the short term. Thus, East Asia managed to obtain the foreign currencies required. In relation to the above the neoliberals point out the role of the exchange rate policy. Overvalued currencies hamper export growth and indirectly slow down the possibility to obtain foreign exchange to meet debt service obligations.

3.2 The causes of the crisis according to the structuralists

According to the structuralists, the African crisis is very much the result of external factors and an unfavourable initial situation at the start of African independence. Moreover, they point out a number of structural bottlenecks in African economies. They also doubt the positive effects of increasing prices on production and the advantages of a development policy aimed at exporting. As was already described in Chapter 1, the structuralists argue in favour of import substitution – especially in the early stages of economic development. The structuralists dismiss the neoclassical trade theory.

On the basis of the structuralists theory, too, many of the facts presented in Chapter 2 may be explained.

The crisis in the agricultural and industrial sector and a decrease in the share of export

In contrast to the traditional structuralists (see Chapter 1), many structuralists today acknowledge the importance of a thriving agricultural sector. The structuralists, too, regard the crisis in the agricultural sector as one of the causes of the current poor economic situation in Africa. However, they believe that the poor development of the agricultural sector and the allied decreasing share in the world market is first and foremost the result of developments which are hardly influenced, if at all, by domestic policy designers. They point out that the world trade system is unfavourable to Africa: the structural decreasing relative prices of agricultural goods on the world market (decreasing terms of trade), the global depression, and the protectionist agricultural policy in industrialised countries. The structuralists believe that the negative terms of trade effect outweighs the possible positive effects of trade on production. Such a process is termed immiserizing growth. Furthermore, they feel that the causes of slight economic progress are very likely the unfavourable weather conditions (long periods of drought), the poor quality of farmland, the widespread existence of smallholders who are merely self-supporting and who react differently to economic incentives than more developed farmers, poor infrastructure, and traditional methods of agriculture that are characterised by low productivity. The structuralists also stress the negative effects of the low diversification of Africa's exports which causes Africa to be rather sensitive to developments on the world market. In contrast to the neoliberal economists – who consider a limited diversification of exports to be the result of a wrong system of stimulating on the part of the African authorities – the structuralists feel that this limited diversity was inherited from Africa's colonial occupation. Colonialism led to large-scale, non-productive plantations. Favouring large-scale agricultural enterprises and plantations is also the result of Africa's domestic policy. Most of the time government expenditure, subsidies for inputs, and access to credit were applied only for the benefit of large enterprises. Smallholders were intentionally put at a disadvantage. Structuralists claim that this affected adversely income distribution, productivity, and the environment. Many smallholders went bankrupt, and at the same time large-scale, commercial agricultural enterprises came into being.

The crisis in the industrial sector shares many of the sources of the crisis in the agricultural sector. In this context too, poor infrastructure is mentioned as well as the unfavourable world trade system, and the colonial inheritance. Colonialism is supposed to be the cause of the fact that African industries are too dependent on capital stock, Western technology and skilled labour. The structuralists also point out the adverse effects of the extreme political instability caused by the diverse cultural backgrounds of the African population – also the result of the colonial division of Africa – the disastrous effects of the debt crisis, and the decrease in international capital flows to Africa (see below).

The low volume and efficiency of investment

According to structuralists, the low efficiency of investment is very much the result of poor infrastructure and traditional methods of production.

The small volume of domestic savings

The small potential of savings in the private sector explains the small volume of private savings in Africa. In Africa incomes are simply too low to cause an increase in savings. After all, savings can be generated only if one temporarily refrains from consumption. Structuralists doubt whether free development of the interest rate – as suggested by the neoliberals – will affect favourably total domestic savings and investment. In this context they point out the large-scale, informal financial market in Africa. Because of the importance of the informal financial sector in Africa it is interesting to consider this sector in greater detail.

Informal credit markets

Informal finance consists of all financial activities that lie beyond the control of the official sector. Other terms used in the literature are: the 'curb', 'parallel', 'underground', or 'unorganized' markets. Montiel *et al.* (1993) distinguish four types of informal financial institutions.

The first type is called occasional lending. It consists of lending by individuals and institutions with a temporary surplus of funds. In most cases the lenders are friends, neighbours and/or close relatives to the borrower. Money is provided on a non-commercial basis with no interest or collateral charged. Loans are provided on the basis of reciprocity: the current lender receives the possibility to borrow in the future from the current borrower. According to Adams (1991) this type of informal finance is probably one of the most important. In some countries informal loans made by friends and relatives make up more than half of all informal loans.

The second type is the so-called regular moneylending by individuals or institutions that specialise in lending. This group consists of moneylenders (in Africa they are called 'katapila'), pawnbrokers and all kinds of sophisticated but unregulated institutions, such as mobile banking. In general, moneylenders use their own funds to extend credit to a relatively small group of borrowers. However, borrowing from the formal sector also exists. In most cases, collateral is not demanded, while the interest rates are relatively high. The moneylender usually lends to investors with whom he or she has personal connections. Pawnbrokers are a special category of moneylenders. They lend only in exchange for valuables provided as collateral. Pawnbroking is not a strict credit transaction, since the item that is used as collateral is sold to the pawnbroker and bought back afterwards. In addition to moneylenders and pawnbrokers, all kinds of unregulated institutions emerge which act like normal banks but are not regulated. An important example is the mobile banker, which in Africa is sometimes called the 'single collector susu system'. In this system mobile bankers regularly visit their clients, usually traders, and collect funds. After some time period the savings, less an agreed sum, are returned. Hence, instead of earning interest on deposits, the saver pays a service. The advantage for the depositor is the access to credit for various purposes.

The third type of informal financial lending considered is called tied credit. In this case the main activity of the lender does not refer to credit activities. Credit is extended between individuals who have a continuing relationship in some other way. An important example of this form of credit relationship is the situation in which landlords provide credit to their tenants.

The fourth type distinguished is group lending. The most important example of this type of lending is the ROSCA, which is a 'rotating savings and credit association' consisting of a small, homogeneous group of members who share a basis of common trust. In most cases, they are from one family or from one village. Each member of the group periodically deposits a small amount of money in a common pool. On rotation, the members have the opportunity to borrow the total sum of money saved. Especially in African countries, where they are called 'tontines', ROSCAs are important. In Africa ROSCAs and fixed-fund associations (see below) are found in nearly half of the existing countries (Miracle *et al.*, 1980, p. 703). In addition to the ROSCAs, there also exist credit groups in which the periodically collected funds are not distributed on rotation between the members. These groups are called savings groups or fixed-fund associations. Members of fixed-funds associations also periodically give funds to a treasury. Sometimes the fixed fund association has only a savings function.

The structuralists claim that in Africa the informal financial sector is much more important for the financing needs than the formal banks. Although precise estimates of the size of the informal financial sector for Africa as a whole do not exist, the share of informal finance in total finance seems to range from about one-third to about three-quarters (Montiel *et al.*, 1993, p. 17). Miracle *et al.* (1980, pp. 701–2) state that 'the great bulk of the African population makes little or no use of formal savings and lending institutions. There are few banks in most areas, and those that are found are either not available to, or if available not used by, the majority of the population for a variety of reasons.' Especially in rural areas there is a total lack of formal banks. Aryeetey and Hyuha (1991) survey research on the informal financial sector in Ghana, Malawi, Senegal, Tanzania and Zaïre and supply estimates of the size of the informal financial sector in these countries. In Ghana informal saving and borrowing mobilisation occurs especially by means of the 'susu system'. It is estimated that more than 75 per cent of all savers in the largest centres of Ghana save via the susu system and that this by means of the susu system was most important. For Malawi the informal financial sector is estimated to be three times as large as the formal financial sector. Informal finance especially takes place via moneylenders, ROSCAs and friends or neighbours. With respect to Senegal, Tanzania and Zaïre there are no estimates of the size of the informal financial sector. However, it seems to be very important, since in all of these countries more than 60 per cent of the population (for Zaïre even more than 85 per cent) earn their living primarily in the informal sector. In these three countries informal financial institutions consist of ROSCAs, fixed-fund associations, friends, moneylenders and landlords.

Traditionally, the informal lenders are associated with monopolistic moneylenders who exploit the poor by charging usurious interest rates and are stereotyped as being exploitative. In this view informal financial intermediation is highly inefficient and costs are high so that a substantial part of total saving goes to informal banks as a reward for the services supplied. Moreover, links between the informal financial market and the official markets are assumed to be weak and informal financial loans are considered to be of a short-term nature. Wai (1977), for instance, suggests that approximately one-third of the demand for informal credit is for 'non-productive' purposes. On the basis of this traditional view, neoliberals argue that an increase in the formal interest rate leads to an increase in funds available for investment. They assume that an increase in the interest rate does not affect the supply of credit from the informal sector due to weak linkages between the formal and informal financial sectors.

However, many recent studies argue that the informal financial market is a highly efficient competitive market with developed linkages with the official markets (e.g. Von Pischke *et al.*, 1983). Based on this 'modern' view, structuralists feel that releasing formal interest rates, as proposed by the neoliberals, will only have as a result that funds, which used to be channelled by means of the informal financial market, are now channelled through the formal market. The structuralists argue that it is highly questionable whether this will lead to an increase in the amount of funds available for investment, as is claimed by the neoliberals. A decrease of the funds available is indeed one of the possibilities since there are more reserve obligations on the formal financial market,[3] that is only part of the funds flowing from the informal to the formal market are actually available for investment.

A decrease in the real foreign capital inflow

According to the structuralists, the decrease in capital inflow is an important source of the present-day African crisis. They stress the adverse effects of the decrease in real foreign capital flows to Africa during the 1980s. This decrease results in many countries being unable to finance the necessary intermediate imports, which in turn affects unfavourably the volume and efficiency of investment and thus industrial and agricultural production. The decrease in the real value of foreign capital flows is not so much the result of a poor African policy but rather of the fact that the international banking system quite abruptly stopped being interested in Africa and of the decreasing contributions of international financial institutions and foreign authorities.

Extensive debt service

Like the decreasing foreign capital flows to Africa, the debt crisis is also considered to be an important source of the current African crisis. The structuralists believe that the debt crisis is not so much the result of domestic factors but rather of external developments. In this context they point out the oil crises of 1973–74 and 1979–80, the global depression in the early 1980s, and the increasing interest rates on the international capital markets.[4]

Before discussing several empirical studies into the causes of the African crisis, I should like to point out an additional source of the crisis that is traditionally excluded from the structuralist and neoliberal analyses but that can be observed in almost all studies into the causes of the crisis in Africa: the high population growth. As mentioned in Chapter 2, population growth in Africa is much higher than in other developing regions. If population growth remains at its present level, it will be extremely difficult actually to realise a per capita rise of the level of prosperity.

3.3 Several empirical studies into the causes of the crisis in Africa

The previous sections have shown that the structuralists and the neoliberal economists hold different opinions on the causes of the present-day crisis in Africa. Empirical studies, in principle, should be able to tell us who is right. However, few empirical studies of Africa have been conducted. Generally, these empirical studies are restricted to the past decades. This means that colonialist influence and the allied division of Africa are paid hardly any attention, if at all. In the case where attention is paid to the influence of colonialism, however, these studies are quite often rather theoretical and descriptive.

A very interesting recent example of such a descriptive study is Davidson (1993), who claims that the current crisis in Africa is primarily a result of the process of nation-building based on European models, and not on Africa's own history. This process of nation-building has its roots in the years of colonialism and is continued by the African political leaders after Africa's independence. The independence of Africa has not led to a restoration of Africa to its own history but has led to European-like states based on colonial partition. Davidson (1993) argues that the strive for nation-statism resulted in fragile societies, in which rulers of the countries do not have vital links with the majority of the population, leading to political and social-economic crises.[5]

Data – figures – on the degree in which colonialism contributed to the current crisis in Africa are, however, hard to find. In other words, recent studies do not provide a definite answer to the structuralist claim that Africa's unfavourable original situation is one of the sources of the present crisis. Besides, cultural and political factors, such as extreme political instability, are not included in the analysis generally. Empirical studies mainly refer to the general question whether domestic or foreign factors have caused the economic crisis; in this context attention is paid only to a subgroup of factors that is of importance, for example, advantages or disadvantages of an export promotion strategy or an import substitution policy, the effects of protectionism in the West, the effects of the development of the terms of trade, and the influence of exchange rate policy. These studies offer a better understanding of the causes of the crisis. It does not provide us with a universal statement, though.

The general impression from these empirical studies is that domestic factors rather than foreign factors have been the main cause of the African economic crisis. Elbadawi *et al.* (1992, p. 15) present a survey of empirical studies into the causes of the crisis in Africa and they conclude that:

> There is no doubt that the sources of the crisis in Africa are multi-dimensional. However, most recent empirical studies point to the importance of inappropriate domestic policies behind the economic malaise in Africa.

To a certain extent this confirms the basic neoliberal principles. There seems to be some consensus on the advantages of an outward-oriented trade policy which is preferred over an inward-oriented policy of import substitution. In general, a positive correlation can be discerned between economic growth and trade orientation.[6] Countries that pursued an outward-oriented policy achieved better economic results than countries that pursued a policy of import substitution. One of the most important reasons for this is the fact that in most developing countries the domestic market is too small to successfully pursue a policy of import substitution. However, there are some important critics of this notion. Michaely (1977) shows that there is only a positive correlation between export orientation and economic growth in the more developed countries. According to Michaely, there is no correlation in the least developed countries. He concludes that economic growth is influenced positively by export orientation only after a certain level of economic development has been reached. Helleiner (1986), too, observes that the positive relation between export orientation and economic growth is based mainly on studies that refer to relatively developed countries. With respect to the least developed countries there are hardly any studies that can confirm the positive relation between export orientation and economic growth. His empirical study suggests that there is no relation between export orientation and economic growth in the case of Africa. More important to an increase of economic growth is the stability of the volume of imports. Helleiner's empirical study actually points to a significant, negative relation between instability of imports and economic growth. Finally, a study by Berthelemy and Varoudakis (1994) is worth mentioning. These authors show that a policy of trade openness has favourable effects only in countries with a developed financial system. In countries where the financial system is underdeveloped, that is in most African countries, trade openness did not exert a positive effect on economic growth. The reason for this is very simple. According to the neoclassical trade theory, trade mainly affects economic growth via a more efficient reallocation of production factors. However, in the case where the financial system is poorly developed this reallocation of production factors is hampered considerably.

In many African countries one of the elements of import substitution policies was to consciously maintain overvalued currencies with a view to lowering the price of the imports required and thus to stimulating the industries. Many recent studies show – on the basis of empirical results – that overvalued currencies are important in explaining the crisis in the agricultural sector in Africa.[7]

On the basis of the supposed advantages of outward-oriented policies, the traditional structuralist argument that an outward-oriented strategy is unfavourable, mainly due to the ever-deteriorating terms of trade, is rejected. If any conclusion can be drawn with respect to the development of the terms of trade, it must be that the terms of trade does not show a systematically increasing or decreasing tendency. Africa's 1960 terms of trade index of 105 rose to 142 in 1980, and dropped to 84 in 1990 (Table 3.4). Africa was faced with a negative development of world prices during the 1980s. However, the deterioration of the terms of trade in this period of time was only slightly less substantial than the improvement of the terms of trade in the previous period.[8] In this context, however, I should refer to the fact that the differences per product – which are not expressed in the aggregate figure – are considerable. Between 1970 and 1990 there was a substantial improvement of the terms of trade for oil, which Nigeria in particular profited of, whereas the terms of trade for minerals and agricultural products deteriorated strongly during this period (Husain, 1993, p. 5). The world market prices of exports significant to Africa – coffee, cocoa, copper, cotton, tea, sugar and tobacco – dropped strongly during the 1980s. In comparison to 1950 the deteriorating terms of trade for these products was between 25 and 60 per cent (Elbadawi *et al.*, 1992, p. 76). Despite the fact that some countries were severely struck by the drop in the world market price of their (most important) exports, most recent studies argue that it is unfair to regard the price movement on the world market as the most important source of the poor export results or of the African crisis as a whole. It is rather revealing that many developing countries outside Africa, for example the Asian developing countries, were also faced with highly deteriorating terms of trade but that these countries did manage to achieve good export results. Many feel that the decrease in Africa's export share, together with a comparable increase in Asia's export share, shows that Africa's government policy is the most important source of the poor export results. Svedberg (1991) agrees with this notion. He has calculated that the decrease in the volume of export, rather than the deteriorating terms of trade, was most important to the decrease in revenues from export.

Empirical studies also contradict the structuralist argument that the agricultural crisis is very much the result of a protectionist policy in the West. A study by Erzan and Svedberg (1989) presents an analysis of the degree to which Africa was struck by protectionist measures (Table 3.5). They distinguish tariff-related and non-tariff-related restrictions.[9] Most African countries are affected by tariff-related restrictions to a small degree. On the European Union (EU, formerly the EC) market, where

Table 3.4 Movements of terms of trade (1987 = 100)

	1960	1967	1971	1980	1986	1991
Africa	105	124	128	142	127	84
Asia	105	100	96	128	104	98
Latin America	95	100	100	157	133	94
Ghana	—	119	94	118	103	62
Ivory Coast	—	107	100	114	120	67
Kenya	—	117	101	124	137	87
Madagascar	—	109	106	95	132	85
Nigeria	—	81	37	186	83	82
Tanzania	—	108	111	112	116	84

Source: Akiyama and Larson, 1994; World Bank, 1989, 1993b

Note: The regional data for 1991 refer to 1990.

Africa sells over 50 per cent of its exports, there are no tariff restrictions for African products, and in the USA and Japan, tariffs are low. The low tariffs are the result of dropping tariffs that were implemented in the industrialised countries in the postwar period. However, they are also the result of the preferential treatment many African countries receive under the terms of the Lomé Conventions[10] and the tariff preferences systems that apply to developing countries which cause tariffs for the group of developing countries as a whole to be much higher than tariffs for Africa. Moreover, in general there are fewer non-tariff-related restrictions for African exports than for exports from other developing countries. Nevertheless, the non-tariff-related restrictions are substantial: over 20 per cent of the value of EU imports from Africa is hindered by non-tariff-related restrictions one way or another. These restrictions mainly refer to agricultural products within the scope of the EU common agricultural policy.

The above analysis does not tell us much about the results of the protectionist measures for Africa. Considering those studies into the effects of liberalisation of agricultural policy in developed countries on developing countries will provide us a better understanding of the issue.[11] The IMF (1992) presents a summary. The studies presented in IMF (1992) distinguish between the effects of liberalisations in the industrialised countries only, and the effects of liberalisations in both industrialised and developing countries. It appears that results differ substantially per study. Still, a general tendency can be discerned. Abolishing protectionist measures in the agricultural policies of developed countries does have a favourable effect on Africa. This effect is smaller than in other developing regions, however, since abolishing protectionist measures means that the preferential treatment of Africa is nullified. One study even concludes that the protectionist measures in the developing countries have a net positive effect on Africa, because Africa could gain an advantage on the market in comparison to many other regions due to this preferential treatment. The studies also conclude that the effects of agricultural liberalisations are far more substantial when

Table 3.5 Protection from the EC, Japan and the USA

	EC Tariffs	EC NTR	Japan Tariffs	Japan NTR	USA Tariffs	USA NTR
Africa	0.01	23	1.64	17	0.48	2
LDCs	1.76	29	4.03	8	6.67	14
Ghana	0.00	0	0.40	9	0.00	0
Ivory Coast	0.00	2	0.20	0	0.10	2
Kenya	0.00	12	3.10	10	0.60	0
Madagascar	0.00	7	1.60	73	0.00	7
Nigeria	0.00	0	2.60	86	0.70	0
Tanzania	0.00	7	0.20	12	0.40	0

Source: Erzan and Svedberg, 1989

Notes: Tariffs = trade weighted average tariffs that Africa and other developing countries are faced with. LDCs = all developing countries. Regional data refer to average actual tariffs in 1983, including preferences, for all exports of the regions, excluding oil. Data for the isolated countries refer to actual tariffs in 1986, including preferences. NTR = non-tariff-related restrictions, measured by the trade coverage ratio, which is the value of imports struck by non-tariff-related restrictions divided by total imports. Quotas on oil are not included.

protectionism by developing countries is reduced, since production will increase due to the advantage of efficiency in a more market-oriented policy.

Finally, I shall briefly discuss the degree to which African farmers respond to price incentives. A positive response to price incentives is one of the basic principles of the neoliberals. The structuralists doubt the positive effects of price rises on an increase in agricultural production. I should mention that on this issue, too, there is a lack of empirical studies. Moreover, most studies refer to one single product, one single country, or even one particular region in a country. One of the few studies conducted in this field is by Bond (1983). He calculated the degree to which price incentives are responded to in nine African countries. It appears that, especially in the short run, elasticities of supply, that is the degree to which price incentives are responded to, are low. This seems to be a rejection of the neoliberal principle.

Still, it is obvious that the above studies do not provide us with any definite answers to the sources of the African crisis. In addition to the restrictions of the empirical studies, which were mentioned in the introduction to this section, I need to point to some other problems. Many statements on the desirability of a certain policy in Africa – especially those that refer to the advantages of an export-oriented policy – are based on studies of the sources of the success in Asian countries. Of course, Africa may learn from this. Nevertheless, there is no way for us to know whether the policy that was successful in Asia will be equally successful in Africa. Mosley (1991) emphasises that the desirability of a certain policy absolutely depends on the stage of development in a particular country. In his point of view, an inward-oriented policy supported by government regulation, tariffs, etc. is conditional upon successful future pursuit of a liberal, export-oriented policy. He also stresses that implementing large-scale liberalisations is disastrous when a country has developed little and is still in the import substitution stage. Mosley (1991, p. 242) states:

> In countries such as Kenya and Malawi it tilted at windmills by asking for liberalisation at a point when the country was still, and rightly, in its inward oriented phase and needed protection before a switch to export-led growth could make any policy sense.

Still, it is not clear whether the above-mentioned favourable results of export-oriented countries are a result of a more liberal domestic policy or rather of a strict government policy which stimulates the exporting sector through export subsidies.

3.4 Summary

The neoliberal economists and the structuralists do not agree at all on the sources of the crisis in Africa. The neoliberal economists, who believe in the beneficial aspects of free markets, emphasise the negative effects of the African government policies. Through regulations, trade restrictions, and by disfavouring the agricultural sector the government hindered Africa's economic progress to a great extent. The neoliberals also stress the disadvantages of large budget deficits. The structuralists, on the other hand, point to the external factors and Africa's poor situation at the start. They do not feel that the crisis is so much a result of the wrong government policy. From their point of view, the government must indeed play an important role in the economy. Many also consider the high population growth to be an important source of the crisis. Purely neoliberal or structuralists notions ignore this factor, though.

It is difficult to prove whether the neoliberals or the structuralists are right. African data are so very inadequate that the outcomes are rather inconsequential. Besides, many of the neoliberal and structuralists statements have not been tested empirically. Very likely the truth lies somewhere in between. The present-day crisis in Africa has both domestic and foreign sources. Still, in recent years the number of advocates of the neoliberal point of view has relatively grown. This is partly the result of the economic studies that point to the great advantages of outward-oriented policies as compared to inward-oriented policies. To some extent, this is the result of those studies that contradict several traditional structuralists arguments, of the disappointing results of Africa and other developing regions that used to pursue a policy based on structuralist notions. For example, many economists now reject the structuralist argument that Africa is faced with ever-deteriorating terms of trade and that the African crisis is very much caused by the protectionist policy pursued in the industrialised countries. Many economists feel that a reduction of Western protectionism and complete liberalisation of the agricultural policy will affect Africa favourably. However, the effects are smaller in Africa than in other developing regions due to the fact that Africa receives a preferential treatment on Western markets. Moreover, the effects of liberalisation in the West appear to be much greater when Africa itself would also reduce its protectionist measures.

Ideological sentiments do play an important part in recent faith in neoliberal measures. Despite reasonable doubt with respect to the degree to which African farmers respond to price incentives, present-day faith in the benefits of free markets and in market incentives is considerable. The World Bank and the IMF, too, have been influenced to a great extent by neoliberal economists. That is why many neoliberal points of view can be discerned in the actual structural adjustment programmes in Africa.

Notes

1 The following description is partly based on Elbadawi *et al.* (1992).
2 The real exchange rate equals the nominal exchange rate corrected for differences between foreign and domestic prices. If the real exchange rate is overvalued, the value of the real exchange rate is too high to realise an equilibrium in the balance of payments, taking into account the 'permanent' volume of foreign capital flows. An overvalued real exchange rate may be the result of an increase in domestic inflation or an appreciation of the nominal exchange rate. Sometimes the real exchange rate is measured as the price of tradable goods in relation to the price of non-tradable goods. In that case, real appreciation is a relative increase of the price of non-tradable goods (see Ch. 6).
3 Commercial banks are obliged to keep part of their means as reserves. They are not allowed to lend these reserves.
4 Hermes (1992) extensively describes the developments in this field.
5 For other studies on the impact of colonialism in Africa see, for example, Chirot (1977) and Amin (1973).
6 See, for example, Balassa (1989), Krueger (1985) and Dollar (1992).
7 Elbadawi *et al.* (1992) present a survey of empirical studies into the influence of overvalued currencies in Africa.
8 According to Husain (1993), who uses different data on the terms of trade, the improvement of the terms of trade during the 1960s and 1970s is even greater than its deterioration during the 1980s.
9 Non-tariff-related restrictions consist, among other things, of quotas, voluntary export restrictions, export subsidies, and quality requirements. Export subsidies play an important role in the agricultural sector with respect to pressurising agricultural prices.
10 At the Lomé Conventions, the European Community and its former colonies reached an agreement on topics such as access to the European market, financial support, etc.
11 See IMF (1992) and Development Committee (1991).

4 The IMF: structure, credit facilities and theoretical framework

The IMF and the World Bank were both founded at Bretton Woods (USA) in July 1944 and are consequently also called the Bretton Woods institutions. The IMF was founded in order to promote international monetary cooperation and stabilisation of exchange rates. The primary role of the IMF is to create a climate in which governments are forced to dismantle restrictions concerning foreign exchange dealings and to promote free trade in goods and capital. From its foundation onwards the IMF mainly concentrated on granting financial support to countries with short-term imbalances in their balance of payments. Promoting development and economic growth was not an explicit IMF objective; this was actually the objective of the World Bank.

At present, the IMF, in cooperation with the World Bank, plays a crucial role in the adjustment programmes in Africa. The IMF extends financial help and technical assistance to those countries that enter into large-scale changes of the structure of their economy. Moreover, the IMF functions as a catalyst in attracting capital from alternative sources like governments and banks.

In Chapters 4, 5 and 6 the role of the IMF and the World Bank in African adjustment programmes will be discussed in detail. In most African countries structural adjustment programmes have been formulated by the IMF in association with the World Bank. It is hard to distinguish between the contributions made by the IMF and the World Bank. In most African countries there is an integrated approach which signifies a consensus between the IMF and World Bank ideas concerning policy conditions which are included in structural adjustment programmes. This is also why I do not distinguish between the IMF and the World Bank when discussing policy conditions of adjustment programmes in Chapter 6. This does not mean that there are no significant differences between the basic ideas of the IMF and the World Bank. This topic will be discussed in detail in Chapters 4 and 5. In these two chapters the structure, the credit facilities, and the traditional analytical framework of the institutions will be the central focus.

The structure of the IMF will be discussed in Section 4.1, the IMF credit facilities in Section 4.2, and the analytical framework of the IMF in Section 4.4. In Section 4.3 I shall discuss the difference between measures aimed at stabilising the economy – which was the original IMF objective – and measures aimed at a structural reform of the economy. Section 4.5 will present a summary of this chapter.

4.1 The structure of the IMF

The IMF is an organisation of a number of countries, its major objective being to improve international monetary cooperation. The highest IMF governing body is the Board of Governors, which consists of governors and deputy governors from each member country. Usually, they are the finance ministers and the presidents of the central banks. The board meets once a year. The governors decide on amendments of by-laws, the entry of new member countries, and increasing the Fund's financial means (Bakker, 1992). Decision-making is based on weighted voting.

The Executive Board is in charge of the day-to-day management of the IMF. It consists of twenty-four governors. Five of them are appointed by individual members – those countries with the largest quotas, i.e. the United States, Great Britain, Germany, France and Japan – and the other governors are appointed by the electoral groups of the remaining member countries. The board is occupied with, among other things, supervising exchange rate policies of member countries, extending financial help to member states, consulting members, and studying important topics. The board appoints a managing director who chairs board meetings and who is in charge of the daily routine at the IMF.

In 1974 two advisory bodies, the Interim Committee and the Development Committee, were founded. The Interim Committee is a temporary advisory body responsible for supervising the management, pursuing adjustments in the international monetary system, and assessing proposals for amendments to by-laws. The ministers from the twenty-four countries on the Executive Board hold seats on this committee. The committee meets twice a year, once in the spring and once just before the annual meeting. The Development Committee, founded by the IMF and the World Bank, is concerned with the IMF and World Bank advice related to the transfer of financial resources to developing countries. The committee consists of twenty-two members – usually the finance ministers of the member countries – who are appointed for a two-year period.

Each member state makes a financial contribution to the IMF, the so-called quota. The quotas of all member states (together with the IMF loans) are paid into a general sources account which provides the IMF with its means. The quotas to a certain extent reflect the impact of member states in the world economy and they are revised every five years. Three-quarters of the contributions consists of the domestic currency of a particular country and the remaining quarter consists of internationally accepted special drawing rights (SDRs).[1] The quota determines the importance of a country's vote, access to financial reserves held by the IMF, and the allocation of new SDRs. Each member country has 250 votes and is appointed extra votes on the basis of the volume of their quota; one extra vote for every 100,000 SDRs of the quota.

4.2 IMF credit facilities

An important part of IMF tasks consists of granting credit to countries that have (temporary) problems concerning their balance of payments. The IMF especially developed several credit facilities for these cases. Table 4.1 presents a survey of the credit facilities together with a short description of their characteristics.[2]

The basic credit facility, aimed at solving short-term problems concerning the balance of payments, consists of an unconditional possibility to borrow, the reserve tranche, and four credit tranches. Each credit tranche comprises 25 per cent of the quota and must be repaid within three to five years. The first credit tranche is largely unconditional. In consultation with the IMF the borrowing country has to draw up a policy programme. Withdrawing credit takes place in phases (usually quarterly) and is geared to the degree to which the criteria agreed on are being met. Appeals to higher credit tranches are almost always embedded in a stand-by arrangement. The IMF issues the majority of its credits under stand-by arrangements. The planned period of a stand-by arrangement is usually a year to a year and a half. The intentions with respect to policy are formulated – in detail – in a letter of intent. This letter reflects the outcome of the policy-related discussions between the member state and the IMF. The IMF can assess the outcomes of the policy of the member state through this letter of intent. The IMF formulates certain target values in order to determine

Table 4.1 IMF credit facilities

Facility	Conditionality	Max. appeal in % of quota	Term of repayment	Year of introduction
Basic credit facility				
reserve tranche	none	25	—	1952
1st credit tranche	adjustment efforts	25	3.25–5 years	1952
higher credit tranches	letter of intent	3*25	3.25–5 years	1952
Extended fund facility (EFF)	medium long period	68 per year 300 cumulative	4.5–10 years	1974
Compensatory facility (CCFF)	cooperation with IMF	95	3.25–5 years	1963
Buffer stock financing facility	cooperation with IMF	35	3.25–5 years	1963
Structural adjustment facilities				
SAF	PFP	50	5.5–10 years	1986
ESAF	PFP	190	5.5–10 years	1988

Sources: Bakker, 1992; IMF Survey, October 1993

whether the adjustment programme of a country functions properly and to indicate possible corrective measures. If a country does not comply with these target values, further granting of credit by the IMF will be impossible.

Credit from basic credit facilities is granted in a special way. A country will borrow by exchanging its domestic currency for foreign currencies or SDRs, that is by buying foreign currencies or SDRs. This is also known as a 'drawing on the IMF'. After a certain period of time, a country will have to buy back the domestic currency with the foreign currency or the SDRs. The IMF charges interest on the drawings. The IMF requests member states that have a strong balance of payments and strong reserves to exchange the domestic currency of their quota for the currency appointed by the IMF. Thus these member states obtain claims on the IMF. In order to guarantee the liquidity of these claims on the Fund, the IMF credit facility needs to have a relatively short term, that is at least with respect to the basic credit facility (Bakker, 1992).

The extended fund facility (EFF) has been designed for the benefit of countries with structural imbalances in production and trade (Bakker, 1992). The introduction of this facility in 1974 signified more IMF attention for long-term supply-side factors of adjustment. Member states can appeal to this facility under an extended arrangement. This means that for the entire three-year period a programme with objectives and intended policy must be drawn up. In addition, an annual letter of intent is to be drawn up. Drawings under the terms of the EFF take place quarterly if target values are met; the term of repayment is four and a half to ten years. The maximum appeal to this facility is reached when drawings under the EFF and the higher credit tranches together amount to 68 per cent of the annual qouta and to 300 per cent cumulatively.

The compensatory and contingency financing facility (CCFF) aims at supporting member states that have difficulties with respect to their balance of payments due to a temporary fall in revenues from exports. These are mainly countries which export raw materials and which are faced with setbacks in exports due to factors external to the country (Bakker, 1992). Since 1981 countries can also borrow to pay for large cost increases of corn imports. Since 1988 compensation for unforeseen circumstances (contingencies) is possible under certain conditions. The reason for this is that member countries must be able to pursue a programme agreed on even when unexpected difficulties occur. In practice almost only those countries that already have a conditional agreement with the IMF can appeal to the CCFF (Polak, 1991). Credit limits under these facilities are as follows: 30 per cent of the quota for contingency financing; 30 per cent for disappointing export revenues; 15 per cent for costs of corn imports; and an extra 20 per cent for supplementing the various parts. Repayments must be completed within three and three-quarters to five years (IMF Survey, October 1993).

The Buffer Stock Financing Facility is designed to finance buffer stocks under the terms of the international agreements on raw materials. This facility has been rather neglected since the early 1990s (Polak, 1991).

Structural adjustment facilities (SAFs) have been designed for Low Income Countries. Only those countries that are eligible for IDA support (International

Development Association, a subdivision of the World Bank) also qualify for SAF and enhanced structural adjustment facility (ESAF) programmes. This means that only the very poorest countries qualify for support from the structural adjustment facilities. Moreover, countries in general cannot appeal to IMF (and World Bank) structural adjustment funds until after they have participated in a short-term adjustment programme through a stand-by arrangement. Soft loans are issued and must be repaid within a certain period of time. Since March 1994 78 countries can appeal to ESAF funds (IMF Survey, 7 March 1994). The structural adjustment facility was established in 1986, the enhanced structural adjustment facility in 1987. The aim of these facilities is to help countries create the conditions for sustained economic growth, to improve their balance of payments, to improve relationships with creditors, and to remove trade and payment restrictions (IMF Survey, October 1993). The interest rate on loans under both SAF and ESAF is 0.5 per cent nominal per annum whereas market interest rates have to be paid on all other facilities. With respect to SAF and ESAF a policy framework paper (PFP) is to be drawn up. A PFP is written by the IMF and the World Bank in close cooperation with the recipient country. However, it is quite obvious that the IMF and World Bank influence is rather substantial (Taylor, 1993, p. 41). In a PFP the authorities present a broad survey of their macroeconomic policy and the adjustment programme for the next three years. In the PFP the most important impediments of increasing growth and improvement of the external payments positions are indicated. Furthermore, it describes the investment programme, the financial requirements, and the role of the main donor countries. Finally, the PFP mentions the social consequences and possible measures to protect the vulnerable groups. The PFP is revised annually. In addition to the PFP, an annual letter of intent – a detailed programme for the next twelve months – is also drawn up. SAF loans are issued once a year, and ESAF loans once every six months. Therefore, within the framework of the SAF, the IMF cannot put pressure on a country that does not perform satisfactorily until negotiations on the next letter of intent are entered into, while it can exert pressure every six months under the terms of the ESAF. Moreover, there is also a difference with respect to conditionality. The contents of SAF arrangements are less specified than the contents of an ESAF programme. In general, only those countries the Fund actually expects to be able to perform properly are granted access to the ESAF. Weaker countries obtain access to smaller credit, which is available under the terms of SAF. The maximum appeal to the SAF is 50 per cent of the quota – 15, 20 and 15 per cent, respectively, in the first, second and third year; the maximum appeal to the ESAF is 190 per cent (in exceptional cases 255 per cent). The total amount of credit available under the terms of the SAF is 2.7 billion SDR and under the terms of the ESAF 6 billion SDR. Until 31 August 1993 1.5 billion SDR of the SAF and 3.2 billion SDR of the ESAF had been granted. In both cases the term of repayment is five and a half to ten years in half-yearly instalments. The ESAF arrangement expired on 30 November 1993. The executive board decided to prolong the ESAF arrangement. Together with the members countries they agreed on opening a capital account of 5 billion SDR and a subsidy account of 2 billion SDR.

A specification of SAF and ESAF arrangements is presented in Table 4.2. A survey

Table 4.2 SAF and ESAF loans until 31 December 1994 (millions of SDRs)

	Stand-by	SAF	ESAF
Africa	3175	1210	2824
Ghana	82	130	389
Ivory Coast	423	—	333
Kenya	85	99	307
Madagascar	43	46	77
Nigeria	969	—	—
Tanzania	64	75	182

Source: IMF Survey, various editions

of the year of introduction and the credit agreed on for adjustment programmes in all African countries is shown in Table A4.1 in the appendix to this chapter. Table 4.2 also shows the credits that Africa has been offered through stand-by arrangements. These figures refer to the total for the July 1986 to January 1994 period.

The table shows that the total amount of loans issued through the SAF and ESAF are now even more important than the stand-by arrangements, that is loans from the basic credit facility. Moreover, Africa was granted a far larger share of SAF and ESAF funds in comparison with other developing regions. The total amount of SAF and ESAF funds for Africa was 4000 million SDRs, while that for East Asia, South Asia and Latin America until the end of 1994 was about 60, 1500 and 300 million SDRs, respectively for these regions (IMF Survey, various issues). The six African countries I selected were granted about 30 per cent of SAF funds and about 45 per cent of ESAF funds for Africa. Ghana in particular received considerable financial aid.

4.3 Stabilisation versus structural reforms

Financial aid granted by the IMF involves conditions with respect to the recipient country's policy. Until the early 1980s the conditions drawn up by the IMF especially referred to short-term stabilisation of the economy. Roemer and Radelet (1991) describe stabilisation as a recovery of the imbalances in the balance of payments, a decrease of government deficits and a decrease of the money supply in order to control inflation and decrease macroeconomic instability. The most important elements of a standard set of stabilisation measures would be:

1 a decrease in the deficits in the balance of payment by a devaluation of the currency
2 reduction of budget deficits by raising taxes, reforming the tax system, and cutting government expenditure
3 restructuring of foreign debts

4 an increase in financing government deficits by means of borrowing on the capital market (issuing government debentures) at the expense of government loans from the central bank (monetary financing)
5 increasing interest rates (in order to increase savings), increasing food prices (in order to decrease the expense of subsidies), and increasing the price to be paid for public services
6 decreasing wages
7 restricting domestic credit.

After a stabilisation programme has been pursued, the structural reform of the economy can be entered into. Structural reforms are reforms aimed at changing the structure of production and consumption and increasing the efficiency and flexibility of the economy. A standard reform 'package' would comprise the following elements (Roemer and Radelet, 1991):

1 liberalisation of markets in order for prices to be determined by supply and demand so that they actually reflect the degrees of scarcity (letting markets work and getting prices right)
2 privatisation of public enterprises
3 an increase of the efficiency of government tasks that are not privatised
4 institutional reforms such as creating new financial institutions.

The measures for stabilising the economy differ from measures aimed at realising a structural reform of the economy. Structural reform measures are directed towards improving the medium and long-term production through changing the structure of the economy whereas stabilisation measures aim at remedying short-term imbalances in the balance of payments by means of restricting the domestic demand.

Despite the fact that it is quite easy to distinguish theoretically between stabilisation and structural reform and despite the fact that they have very different objectives, in actual practice these differences are difficult to discern and the desired measures are often identical. Certain measures are indeed aimed both at stabilising the economy and at structurally reforming the economy. An example may be a devaluation of the currency. The objective of devaluation is to reduce the deficit in the current account in the short term (stabilisation), and at the same time to stimulate economic activities in the exporting sector at the expense of activities in the sector that produces for the domestic market only (structural reform). Other measures, too, such as increasing interest rates, decreasing food subsidies and higher prices for government services can be found in programmes that aim at a structural reform of the economy. The structural adjustment programmes that are currently implemented in Africa include measures that are directed towards both stabilising and structurally reforming the economy (see Ch. 6).

As has been observed earlier, the primary concern of the IMF is stabilisation of the economy. The stand-by arrangements have been specially designed for this purpose. The member state has to reach such a balance of payments position that a deficit in the current account is lastingly funded by net capital inflows in accordance with the level of development and the growth prospects of the member state. During the 1980s the IMF gradually started paying more attention to the structural causes of deficits in balances of payments. More attention was also paid to the structural causes of the low economic growth and measures that refer to the structural reform of the economy. Although promoting economic growth is not the main concern of the IMF, the SAF and ESAF programmes do concentrate on this to a significant extent. In practice IMF authorities are said to rank growth higher than adjustment (Polak, 1991, p. 19) – which is disputed by IMF critics, though.

4.4 The traditional analytical framework of the IMF

The IMF applies the term of financial programming to describe the process that is completed to determine the policy values of the stabilisation programmes. In this context, the Fund applies macroeconomic models. The initial models – designed in the 1950s and 1960s – started from a monetarist approach of the balance of payments. Below, I shall discuss a slightly different version of one of the IMF models, the model by Polak (1957). Despite the fact that the new models pay more attention to factors that determine economic growth and despite the fact that the IMF uses various models for different situations it is quite useful to consider the Polak model. The Polak model is indeed the basis of almost all IMF models. The model used to be applied to stabilisation programmes. It is not suitable for determining the measures that are needed for a structural reform of the economy. Before a country enters upon a process of structural reform, stabilisation of the economy is a prerequisite in almost all cases. The insights provided by the Polak model, therefore, remain extremely significant to the practical implementation of adjustment programmes. After discussing the model, I will discuss the actual practice of financial programming.

The Polak model

A somewhat adjusted version of the model by Polak can be described by means of five equations.

1 $\Delta M_s = \Delta RES + \Delta DC$

with ΔM_s denoting an increase in the money supply, ΔRES denoting an increase in foreign reserves and ΔDC denoting an increase in the loans from the central bank to the government. Δ indicates a change in a variable at a given moment in time. Thus, ΔM equals the increase in M, i.e. M during period t (M_t) minus M during the period $t-1$ (M_{t-1}), etcetera.

Equation 1 represents the monetary system in a very simple economy.[3] The equation is inferred from the balance of the central bank. On the left-hand side of the equation is the increase in the liabilities of the central bank, on the right-hand side is the increase in the assets of the central bank. The increase in liabilities is assumed to equal the increase in assets. The amount of money in circulation (M) is among the central bank's liabilities for historical reasons. In the past people could go to the central bank and exchange their money for gold. International reserves are the foreign currencies kept by the banking sector. These reserves are claims by the central bank on the foreign central bank. In principle, the central bank could take its foreign currency to a central bank abroad to exchange it for gold (this is no longer possible). It is self-evident that loans from the central bank to the government are assets to the central bank.

Equation 1 may also be interpreted differently. Since the left-hand side of the equation equals the right-hand side, it follows that the amount of money in circulation grows when international reserves and credit loans to the government increase. The supply of international reserves grows due to interventions by the central bank on the currency market. Since foreign currencies are purchased with domestic currency, an increase of the amount of money in circulation is the logical result.[4] An increase in loans by the central bank to the government – monetary financing – increases the domestic money supply because the government uses this money to make payments (e.g. salaries of civil servants) so that the money is put into circulation.

2 $\Delta RES = x - z + \Delta F$

where x denotes exports, z denotes imports, and ΔF foreign capital inflows.

Equation 2 is a simplified representation of the balance of payments of a country. In a balance of payments all foreign transactions of a country are recorded. These transactions consist of exports, imports of foreign goods and services, interest payments, capital inflows, and such inflows as loans and foreign investment. If the total of the balance on the current account (exports of goods and services minus imports of goods and services and net interest payments: represented in a simplified way in equation 2 by $x - z$) and the balance on the capital account (capital inflows minus capital outflows; ΔF in equation 2) is positive, the supply of international reserves (RES) increases. If the total of the balance in the current account and the balance in the capital account is positive – that is there is a surplus in the balance of payments – the inflow of money exceeds the outflow of money so that international reserves increase.

Equations 1 and 2 together show that the amount of money in circulation increases if a country has a surplus in its balance of payments. A surplus in the balance of payments results in an increase of the foreign reserves which, in turn, leads to an increase in the money supply.

3 $Y = Py$

where Y denotes the nominal national income, P is the general price level, and y is the real national income.

Equation 3 presents the value of nominal national income. Nominal income equals real income multiplied by the price level. The basic IMF model assumes that real income (the amount of goods produced) is given, so that changes in nominal income are always the result of a change in prices. This reflects the short-term character of IMF stabilisation programmes: real income, which is determined by the supply of goods, is given.

4 $z_t = 0.2\ Y_t$

Equation 4 is the import equation. It shows that imports increase due to an increase in nominal income. For the sake of convenience, I presuppose imports to equal 20 per cent of nominal income.

5 $\Delta M_s = \Delta Y$

Equation 5 is an extremely simplified representation of the quantity equation.[5] The equation shows that an increase in the nominal income corresponds with an increase in the money supply; and an increase in the money supply results in an increase of nominal income. Since real income is presupposed to be constant, equation 5 suggests that an increase in the money supply results in an increase of prices.

How then does the IMF apply the Polak model in stabilisation programmes? Among other things, a surplus in the balance of payments or a decrease of the deficit in the balance of payments is striven for by means of the stabilisation programmes. As follows from equation 2, a deficit in the balance of payments results in a decrease in the volume of foreign reserves. The IMF sets a limit to the decrease in foreign reserves. Given the estimation made with respect to the volume of exports and foreign capital flows, which are determined outside the model, applying equation 2 one can determine the maximum import with the desired increase of international reserves. When the maximum import has been determined, equation 4 is used to determine maximum nominal national income. Since real income is constant, the maximum price rise is determined, in accordance with the objective of the balance of payments. Consequently, equation 5 is used to determine the maximum increase in the money supply. Finally, equation 1 is used to determine the maximum domestic credit to the government, after filling in the fixed change in international reserves and the estimation of the related change in the money supply. Thus, maximum domestic credit from the central bank to the government can be determined by estimating in reverse order.

An example may clarify matters: the IMF wants the supply of international reserves to be constant (i.e. an equilibrium in the balance of payments: $\Delta RES = 0$). If exports are expected to be 90 ($x = 90$), and foreign capital flows are 10 ($\Delta F = 10$), equation 2 estimates the maximum volume of imports (z) to equal 100. Consequently, it can be determined from equation 4 that the maximum volume of nominal income is 500. If income in the preceding period was 450, it follows from equation 5 that the maximum increase in the domestic money supply is 50. After filling in this outcome in equation 1 – taking into account the maximum decrease of international reserves – it follows that the maximum volume of credit from the central bank to the government equals 50. It can also be inferred that the maximum volume of loans from the central bank to the government increases to 110 if international reserves are allowed to decrease by 10. Conversely, this example shows that an increase in credit facilities from the central bank to the government results in a stronger decrease in international reserves. Thus, an increase in government credit loans leads to a larger deficit in the balance of payments.

In the Polak model, an increase in domestic credit from the central bank to the government affects nominal national income. As is clearly shown by the above example, an increase in domestic credit involves a decrease in international reserves.

A decrease in international reserves involves an increase of imports and consequently an increase in the nominal national income (see equation 4). Due to the presupposition of a constant real income, prices are indeed also affected positively by an increase in domestic credit. This implies that an increase in domestic credit leads to a deterioration of the balance of payments and a price rise (i.e. inflation). Since the IMF stabilisation programmes are mainly directed towards a recovery of the balance of payments and a decrease of inflation, it is obvious why the IMF sets great store by restricting domestic credit.

Since credit from the central bank to the government especially comes from financing needs caused by government deficits, there is a direct relation between government deficits and deficits in the balance of payments and increasing inflation. An increase in the government deficit leads to an increase in the money supply which, through an increase in income and thus imports, affects the balance of payments (and inflation). Therefore, IMF programmes strive for a decrease in government deficits by means of increasing taxes, decreasing government expenditure (for example, by reducing the salaries for civil servants), decreasing subsidies, and increasing the price of public services (see Section 4.3). It is also clear now why the IMF prefers financing government deficits by issuing government bonds over borrowing from the central bank (monetary financing). For financing government deficits by issuing government bonds does not lead to an increase in the money supply, that is the negative consequences of a government deficit to the balance of payments and inflation need not occur. However, in most African countries there is no market for government bonds so that their only option is to reduce their government deficit.

A variable that is of major importance in IMF stabilisation programmes, but which has not been discussed yet, is the exchange rate. The IMF considers exchange rates to be among the most important policy variables that may be used to improve the balance of payments. According to the IMF, a devaluation of the currency leads to an increase in exports because it will be cheaper for foreign countries to purchase goods. Moreover, a devaluation also results in an increase in the price of imports so that the demand for imports will fall. Both effects affect the balance of payments favourably. On the other hand, another consequence of a devaluation is that a higher price has to be paid for a given volume of imports. This affects unfavourably the balance of payments. The IMF presupposes that the positive effects outweigh the one negative effect so that devaluation of a currency leads to an improvement of the balance of trade and consequently to an improvement of the balance of payments.

Financial programming in practice

Designing a programme is actually much more complicated and pragmatic than the simple model by Polak will cause one to suspect. Financial programming is a cooperative and negotiation process between the IMF and its member states. This process includes the following steps (IMF, 1987; Tarp, 1993):

1 Policy variables are set: usually the desired amount of international reserves, inflation, and additional domestic credit to the private sector.

2 A forecast is produced with respect to exogenous variables. Predictions concerning revenues from exports are made on the basis of predictions concerning the real growth of income on the export market of the country in question and export prices of rival countries on the world market at the present exchange rate. With respect to capital flows, it is necessary to determine the 'permanent' level of foreign debt, that is the debt that is consistent with the present and future prospects of the country to meet its liabilities. Furthermore, the extent of the increase in debt to this particular level can be determined. Capital flows will probably consist of relief flows, direct investment and commercial foreign credit.

3 Initial determination of the value of potential imports; the value that is consistent with the determined change of the amount of international reserves.

4 The value of potential imports (estimated under 3) is usually too low to keep up the level of production since imports often consist of intermediate goods like machinery and oil, which are employed in the production process. Another estimation of exports is made after devaluation, followed by a recalculation of potential imports. If devaluation is impossible, as it is in the African franc zone, variables are treated as being endogenous, for example, by adjusting policy variables or predictions concerning real income or exports.

5 After the imports have been determined, nominal income can be determined. Consequently, the quantity equation is applied in order to determine the demand for money.

6 After having determined the demand for money, the maximum growth of domestic credit is estimated, taking into account the policy variable change in foreign reserves.

7 The outcome under 6 is compared with the total domestic demand for credit, comprising the public and the private demand for credit. The above-mentioned model is extended with the following equation:

$$6 \quad \Delta DC = \Delta DC_g + \Delta DC_p$$

with ΔDC_g and ΔDC_p denoting credit to the government and the private sector, and ΔDC denoting total domestic credit.

Domestic credit to the private sector is usually a policy variable since enterprises should be capable of investing. ΔDC is determined in the above described manner – the only difference being the fact that total domestic credit must now be divided in loans to the government and loans to the private sector. The desired granting of credit to the private sector is subtracted from the estimated maximum total domestic credit; the difference is the maximum amount of credit to the government.

8 An initial calculation of maximum government expenditure by comparing desired government expenditure and expected government receipts and estimated maximum credit to the government. If this estimation is different from the planned budget of the authorities, government consumption, government receipts and/or domestic credit to the government must be adjusted.

9 Negotiations concerning structural adjustment: the spending policy and the various supplies in the economy are likely to be adjusted which in turn will affect

real production. These adjustments may (temporarily) lead to a deterioration of the current account so that additional financing is required.

10 The complete programme will be tested for consistency.

11 The final agreement on implementing the programme and on achievement criteria is laid down in a policy framework paper and/or a letter of intent.

4.5 Summary

The IMF is a monetary institution which traditionally concentrated on short-term stabilisation of the economy. From the early 1980s onwards, however, the IMF also started concentrating on the long-term causes of the economic crisis in developing countries. For this purpose the SAF and the ESAF were designed for countries that wished to introduce a structural adjustment programme. The policy framework paper, laid down by the World Bank and the IMF in association with the developing country in question, is the official adjustment programme to be pursued.

Despite the substantial IMF attention for the structural sources of the crisis, measures for stabilising the economy are of even greater importance in IMF programmes. In practice, structural reform of the economy cannot be implemented until a stabilisation programme has been executed. The IMF developed several models that are employed in the estimation of measures for stabilising the economy. The Polak model has been the basis for these models. This model was especially used to estimate the volume of domestic credit that fits a particular objective concerning the balance of payments. According to the basic IMF model, a deficit in the balance of payments is caused by excessive domestic credit only; therefore, restricting domestic credit ranks high in the traditional IMF stabilisation programmes. Since a considerable part of domestic credit consists of loans to the government for financing their budget deficit, special attention is paid to the necessity of reducing government deficits.

Appendix to Chapter 4: SAF and ESAF loans for Africa

Table A4.1 Year of introduction, and SAF and ESAF loans agreed on (in millions of SDRs, until 31 December 1994)

Countries	SAF	ESAF
Benin	1989 (21.91)	1993 (51.89)
Burkina Faso	1991 (22.12)	1993 (48.62)
Burundi	1986 (29.89)	1991 (42.70)
Cent. Afric. Rep.	1987 (21.28)	
Chad	1987 (21.42)	
Comoros	1991 (3.15)	
Equatorial Guinea	1988 (12.88)	1993 (12.88)
Ethiopia	1992 (49.42)	
Gambia	1986 (10.86)	1988 (20.52)
Ghana	1987 (129.86)	1988 (388.55)
Guinea	1987 (40.53)	1991 (57.90)
Guinea-Bissau	1987 (5.25)	
Ivory Coast		1994 (333.48)
Kenya	1988 (99.40)	1989 (261.40) 1993 (45.23)
Lesotho	1988 (10.57)	1991 (18.12)
Madagascar	1987 (46.48)	1989 (76.90)
Malawi		1988 (66.96)
Mali	1988 (35.56)	1992 (79.24)
Mauritania	1986 (23.73)	1992 (33.90)
Mozambique	1987 (42.70)	1990 (130.05)
Niger	1986 (21.40)	1988 (47.18)
Rwanda	1991 (30.66)	
São Tomé e Principe	1989 (2.80)	
Senegal	1986 (54.04)	1988 (144.67) 1994 (130.79)

Table A4.1 *(Continued)*

Countries	SAF	ESAF
Sierra Leone	1986 (40.53)	
	1994 (27.02)	
Somalia	1987 (30.94)	
Tanzania	1987 (74.90)	1991 (181.90)
Togo	1988 (26.88)	1989 (46.08)
		1994 (65.16)
Uganda	1987 (69.72)	1989 (219.12)
		1994 (120.51)
Zaïre	1987 (203.70)	
Zimbabwe		1992 (200.60)

Sources: IMF Survey (various editions)

Note: Frequently, loans are extended in later years. The table shows the amount most recently agreed on. Some countries could draw twice from the ESAF or SAF.

Notes

1 Special drawing rights (SDRs) are international financial reserves created by the IMF. They are allocated to member states on the basis of their contribution. SDRs are based on the composite value of several different currencies and they include the five primary currencies (US dollar, Deutschmark, Japanese yen, French franc and pound sterling). All financial transactions of the IMF are expressed in SDRs. The interest rate the IMF applies is based on a weighted average of interest rates in the five countries of the currencies which together make up the SDRs (Bakker, 1992).

2 A recently developed IMF credit facility is the systemic transformation facility (STF) which was especially designed to help former Eastern Bloc countries during their transition from a planned economy to a market economy. However, this facility is of no importance in Africa and is therefore not included in Table 4.1

3 See also Appendix 2 to Chapter 2.

4 Domestic currency held by the central bank is not included in the domestic currency stock because it is not in circulation.

5 This equation has been inferred after having made use of an equation for the demand for money (which is assumed to depend on nominal income, and a rate of velocity of money with a value of 1) and by presupposing the money supply to equal the demand for money.

5 The World Bank: structure, credit facilities and theoretical framework

Like the IMF, the World Bank was founded at Bretton Woods in July 1944. Contrary to the IMF, the task of the World Bank was to grant financial means for the promotion of long-term economic development and reconstruction. Traditionally, the World Bank mainly concentrated on financing projects. The economic developments during the 1970s and early 1980s, in particular the debt crisis, prompted a major policy review with respect to developing countries. Financing projects proved to be unsuitable to combat stagnating growth. Moreover, the conditions that were involved in this form of lending did not affect the economic variables – e.g. exchange rates, prices of agricultural goods, interest rates, and trade policies – that were considered important to promoting economic growth (Mosley *et al.*, 1991, p. 65). In the early 1980s the World Bank introduced the structural and sectoral adjustment loans (SALs and SECALs), which were aimed at extensive economic reform programmes.

In this chapter I shall discuss the organisation and the structure of the World Bank (Section 5.1), its credit facilities with respect to Africa (Section 5.2) and the structure of the traditional economic models on which World Bank advice is based (Section 5.3). The summary in Section 5.4 will conclude this chapter.

5.1 The structure of the World Bank

The World Bank Group comprises three institutions: the International Bank for Reconstruction and Development (IBRD), commonly known as the World Bank, the International Finance Corporation (IFC) and the International Development Association (IDA). The main objective of these three organisations is to promote economic and social progress in developing countries by increasing economic productivity (Bakker, 1992, p. 53). The World Bank is mainly an investment bank. It also plays an important role as an economic–technical adviser and as a catalyst in initiating capital flows to developing countries.

IBRD credits are granted on business economic conditions. All loans are granted to governments or private institutions backed by the government. The IFC grants loans to and participates in the capital stock of enterprises in developing countries – also without government backing – up to 25 per cent (in Africa 35 per cent) of the costs of the project (Bakker, 1992, p. 67). The special attention for Africa is shown by the attitude of funds like the African Management Service Company which aims at improving the quality of management in African enterprises (Bakker, 1992, p. 69). The IDA issues loans with terms up to fifty years to the poorest countries. The loans are interest-free although administrative charges do have to be paid for. For the first ten years no repayments have to be made. The economic strength and creditworthiness of a country determines whether it will borrow from the IBRD or the IDA. The SALs and SECALs are issued through the IBRD and the IDA.

Countries that wish to become members of the World Bank first have to be members of the IMF. Most IBRD member states are also members of the IFC and the IDA.

The organisational structure of the World Bank is quite similar to that of the IMF. Its highest governing body is the Board of Governors, consisting of governors and deputy governors from each member state. The board meets once a year, in conjunction with the IMF board. The Board of Executive Directors, twenty-three in total, is in charge of day-to-day management of the IBRD, the IFC and the IDA. The five largest shareholders – the United States, the United Kingdom, Germany, France and Japan – each have their own director, the others are appointed by voting groups which represent the remaining member states. Their financial contributions determine the significance of their votes. The number of votes assigned to the African countries I selected are 1106, 2766, 2711, 1048, 7352 and 5903 for Ghana, the Ivory Coast, Kenya, Madagascar, Nigeria and Tanzania respectively. A comparison with the United States, which has 243,359 votes, illustrates that the financial contributions and consequently the number of votes of these countries are extremely small (Rotberg, 1994). The president of the World Bank is the chairman of the Executive Board and also chief of the operating staff. The Development Committee, an advisory organisation to the IMF and the World Bank (already mentioned in Chapter 4) mainly concentrates on World Bank policy. It also assists in creating and coordinating capital flows from other contributors.

Each member state makes a financial contribution to the IBRD, which is raised regularly and of which only a small part is actually paid. The remainder is callable capital which provides the World Bank with a high creditworthiness. The Bank mainly borrows on the international capital markets in order to finance its own loans. IBRD loans involve an interest rate that is 0.5 per cent higher than the finance expenses, that is the IBRD functions as a financial intermediary for cheap credit for developing countries. After all, unlike the World Bank, developing countries cannot borrow at those favourable conditions on the international capital markets. The IDA loans are funded by member states, in particular by industrialised and oil-exporting countries, and to a small extent with IBRD profits.

5.2 World Bank credit facilities

Traditionally, the World Bank mainly concentrated on financing such projects as investment in production capacity and infrastructure. From the early 1980s onwards there has been a shift to programmes that were not related to any project, but to a structural reform of the economy. The SALs and SECALs, which were introduced in 1980 and 1983 respectively, are the primary credit facilities the World Bank designed to support structural reform programmes. The SALs provide medium-term loans (maximum five years) which are to finance reform programmes the borrowing countries have agreed on with the World Bank. The SALs are extensive programmes, which involve numerous conditions which are elaborated on in policy framework papers (PFP). The numerous conditions and the number of parties involved quite often hamper the negotiation process to a large extent. Moreover, often the civil service is incapable – or unwilling – of implementing all conditions. The conditions are not always mutually consistent. The World Bank actually acknowledged these problems concerning SAL arrangements. Therefore, the World Bank introduced SECALs which may be compared with SALs but are less complex. SECALs are directed towards specific activities, usually in particular sectors, so that they suit better those countries that are unable to implement a complete SAL. Between 1984 and 1991 there was a shift from SALs to SECALs. In 1992 this shift was somewhat reversed again: in 1992 26 per cent of all World Bank loans consisted of SALs and 22 per cent of SECALs (Williams, 1994, p. 125).

In 1980 Kenya was the first country to implement a SAL arrangement. Malawi, Mauritius and Senegal followed in 1981. At present, almost all African countries acquired one or several SALs or SECALs. Table A5.1 in the appendix presents a survey of the financial means that have been issued to Africa through SALs and SECALs.

Supplementary to the SALs and SECALs, additional means were provided to Africa to finance the adjustment programmes. In July 1985 the World Bank introduced the Special Facility for Africa for a period of three years. A total of US$2 billion was mobilised by means of this facility (Abbott, 1993, p. 113). It was financed with contributions made by members and the IBRD. The means were especially used for joint credit to those African countries that qualified for IDA credit and that had implemented or would implement a policy reform programme. A total of forty-nine projects divided among twenty-five countries were supported. Ghana was given support for five projects, Madagascar, Niger and Zaïre for three projects, and the remaining countries could (partly) finance one or two projects through this facility (Abbott, 1993, p. 114). The total amount of credit granted through SALs, SECALs and the special facility is presented in Table 5.1.

The nominal volume of adjustment loans to Africa increased during the 1980s. In 1992 the total net capital inflow to Africa amounted to approximately US$17 billion (see Ch. 2) whereas the World Bank adjustment loans amounted to a little over US$1 billion. To some individual countries like Ghana, the Ivory Coast and Kenya, however, the amount is rather substantial. The African countries I selected received over 45 per cent of the total amount of World Bank adjustment loans to Africa.

In 1987 an additional credit facility, the Special Programme of Assistance (SPA), was introduced. The objective of this three-year programme is to support the implementation of policy reform programmes by providing additional concessional finance and by restructuring debts. The extra means are presented as donations or at

Table 5.1 Adjustment loans (millions of dollars)

	1980–82	1983–85	1986–88	1989–91	1992–93	Total
Africa	190	468	1235	1443	1158	12341
Asia	200	383	1130	915	652	7237
Latin America	62	675	2665	2484	1573	18138
Ghana	—	203	303	296	193	995
Ivory Coast	150	250	250	330	450	1430
Kenya	70	131	172	295	201	869
Madagascar	—	60	301	—	3	364
Nigeria	—	250	452	620	—	1322
Tanzania	50	—	96	335	223	704

Sources: World Bank 1992a, 1992b, 1993c

Notes: The amounts include the means available through the Special Facility for Africa. The figures for the regions refer to yearly amounts (with the exception of the total).

conditions no stricter than IDA conditions. In order to qualify for this type of credit, a country not only needs to implement an economic reform programme with the World Bank or the IMF but also must be severely indebted. In October 1992 a third phase was agreed on for the 1994–6 period. The objective is still to support policy reform programmes developed in conjunction with the World Bank and the IMF by providing rapid finance with respect to problems concerning the balance of payments. Under the management of the World Bank, a SPA-3 programme concerning the objectives, priorities and credit conditions for the third phase has been designed (World Bank 1993c, pp. 111–12).

5.3 The traditional analytical framework of the World Bank

The World Bank is a development institution, one of its tasks being to provide foreign financial means that are required for medium- and long-term economic growth. This is in sharp contrast to the IMF which, traditionally, provided only short-term financial relief for solving imbalances in the balance of payments. The World Bank concentrates on providing financial means for investment projects and on promoting long-term economic growth. Therefore, the analytical framework of the World Bank centres around real variables whereas the basic model of the IMF mainly centres around monetary variables.

With a view to the main task of the World Bank, the Revised Minimum Standard Model (RMSM) was designed in 1973. For many years this model was the most influential economic model which formed the basis of World Bank advice (see Addison, 1989; Mills and Nallari, 1992). The RMSM is very much based on the two-gap models which were quite often referred to in debates on developmental policy (see also Chenery and Strout, 1966). These particular models were especially used for calculating the volumes of investment, imports and foreign relief that are required to realise a target growth of gross domestic product.[1]

The RMSM consists of several equations and variables which are applied at a national level. Policy designers determine the desired growth of the domestic product. By means of the RMSM, the imports and investment that are required for the planned growth rate are calculated. By confronting the estimated imports and investment with the planned domestic savings and exports, the savings gap and the trade gap are determined. These values indicate the desired extent of foreign relief and thus of the financial aid to be provided by the World Bank.

Despite attempts to minimise the number of equations in the RMSM, the model comprises about 430 variables for each country. In order to get an idea of the structure of this World Bank model, I shall discuss the most basic form of a two-gap model only.

Most two-gap models make use of the Harrod-Domar production function. A production function reflects the relation between the volume of production factors (for example, capital, i.e. machinery) and production. A Harrod-Domar production function presupposes that production (y) equals the value of capital stock (k) multiplied by capital productivity (v):

1 $y = vk$

Equation 1 presupposes that capital stock actually restricts production. Generally, it is assumed that capital productivity is constant in the course of time. Taking this into account, we can infer from equation 1 that the increase of production (Δy) equals an increase in capital stock (Δk) multiplied by capital productivity:

2 $\Delta y = v\Delta k$

Δ indicates a change of a variable. Since the increase in capital stock per definition equals investment (i), equation 2 can be rewritten as follows:

3a $\Delta y = vi$

or

3b $i = \Delta y/v$

By rewriting equation 3b one can determine the volume of investment required for a desired growth of production. Next, the right-hand side of the equation is multiplied by y/y (i.e. 1):

4 $i = (y/v)\ \Delta y/y = (y/v)\ q$

with q denoting the desired growth rate of production ($\Delta y/y$). The equation shows that required investment increases as a higher growth rate of production is desired and as capital productivity is lower. Thus, the importance of an increase in capital productivity becomes obvious. Policy advice by the World Bank, therefore, was and still is very much concentrated on increasing capital productivity. An increase in capital productivity may be achieved by, for example, improving infrastructure, privatisation, technological improvements, improving the educational system, and tax reforms.

Equation 4 can be used to determine the volume of investment that is required for the desired growth rate of production. For example, the initial value of production (y) is 1000, capital productivity (v) is 0.25, and the production growth that a particular country wants to achieve is 4 per cent ($q = 0.04$). When equation 4 is completed with these figures, investment must be 160 in order to achieve the desired growth of 4 per cent.

Next, an estimation is made of the total ex ante (planned) domestic savings (s_d) of the country in question. The required investment is compared with the ex ante domestic savings. The difference is known as the savings gap. The extent of the savings gap provides an indication of the amount of foreign capital flows (ΔF) that is needed to finance the investment, and thus for the desired growth rate of production. In an equation this reads as follows:

5 $\quad i - s_d = \Delta F$

Equation 5 shows that the required volume of investment can be financed by domestic savings and foreign capital flows (see equation A7b in the appendix to Chapter 2). If ex ante savings are 50, this equation shows that an investment of 160 requires foreign capital inflow to be 110.

In equation 5 it is presupposed that it makes no difference to a country whether investment goods are produced at home or abroad. However, in many developing countries most investment goods are imported. Since these goods are paid for with foreign currency, it is not clear whether domestic savings – expressed in the domestic currency – can be used for this purpose. For this reason the trade gap is also calculated. With the trade gap the amount of foreign currency required for the desired investment is estimated. When it is presupposed that a particular country imports machinery only, the required total import (z) is 128 if 80 per cent of investment must consist of imported machinery:

6 $\quad z = 0.8\, i$

Next, ex ante (planned) export (x) is estimated. The difference between desired imports and planned exports determines the required amount of additional foreign currency.

7 $\quad z - x = \Delta F$

Equation 7 may be compared with equation 2 in Chapter 4. The equation is a simplified representation of one country's balance of payments in which I have abstracted from changes in foreign reserves (see also equation A7a in the appendix to Chapter 2). The difference between import (z) and export (x) is called the trade gap. If planned exports equal 20, a foreign capital inflow of 108 is required, taking into account the desired imports of 128.

I have now applied two different methods to calculate the required foreign capital inflow. The ultimate desired foreign capital inflow is determined by means of the maximum of the calculated values of the trade and savings gaps. In my example, the savings gap provides the highest estimation. The foreign capital inflow – development aid – that is required to achieve a production growth of 4 per cent is therefore calculated to be 110.

However, a well-known economic identity presupposes that the deficit in the trade balance $(z - x)$ per definition equals the difference between investment and savings:[2]

$$8 \quad z - x = i - s_d$$

How then does this equation harmonise with the above determined differences between the trade gap and the savings gap? In order to gain a good understanding, it is important to distinguish between plans and realisations. In retrospect it will appear that the trade gap and the savings gap are identical. However, the above calculated trade gap and savings gap made use of planned exports and savings. If a country acquires the desired foreign capital inflow of 110, it will appear that not all plans can be realised. Foreign capital inflow of 110 plus export revenues (20) will lead to the country in question obtaining foreign currencies of 130 whereas it wishes to spend only 128 on imports.[3] The surplus value of 2 can be eliminated by decreasing export to 18. The country may also decide to import more than it considers necessary. In both cases, the actual difference between imports and exports equals the difference between investment and domestic savings.

The RMSM centres on the real sector of the economy. Paramount are the calculations of real investment, real imports, and real production (if capital inflow is given). A significant deficiency is that no attention whatsoever is paid to monetary variables, like forces that determine prices. The emphasis the World Bank currently places on structural adjustment loans as part of the adjustment programmes requires an adjustment of the RMSM. Therefore, extensions of the RMSM have been developed recently; these are the so-called RMSM-X and RMSM-XX models which will eventually result in the MACOR model.[4]

5.4 Summary

The principal aim of the World Bank – comprising the International Bank for Reconstruction and Development (IBRD), the International Finance Corporation (IFC) and the International Development Association (IDA) – is to promote economic growth in developing countries. In the past, the realisation of this objective was mainly pursued by means of project lending. By introducing SALs and SECALs, the World Bank shifted its attention to programme lending which involves numerous conditions with respect to the economic policy of developing countries.

The current emphasis on programme lending demanded an adjustment of the basic model the World Bank used to apply in policy recommendations. The traditional economic World Bank model was strongly based on two-gap models which mainly centre on the real sector of the economy. The model was especially used for estimating the financial means that are required to achieve a certain economic growth. In current economic World Bank models far more attention is paid to domestic monetary variables. The traditional model is extended with aspects from the IMF programme lending model. Thus, the World Bank deviates from its original policy.

Appendix to Chapter 5: SALs and SECALs for Africa

Table A5.1 SALs and SECALs for Africa (millions of dollars)

Country	1980–82	1983–85	1986–88	1989–91	1992–93	Total
Benin	—	—	—	100	—	100.00
Burkina Faso	—	—	—	80	28	108.00
Burundi	—	—	121	33	30	184.00
Cameroon	—	—	—	150	—	150.00
Cent. Afric. Rep.	—	—	85	45	—	130.00
Chad	—	—	—	98	—	98.00
Comoros	—	—	—	8	—	8.00
Congo	—	—	70	—	—	70.00
Ethiopia	—	—	—	—	250	250.00
Gabon	—	—	50	—	—	50.00
Gambia	—	—	17	23	—	40.00
Ghana	—	203	303	296	193	995.00
Guinea	—	—	107	20	—	127.00
Guinea-Bissau	—	15	15	23	—	53.00
Ivory Coast	150	250	250	330	450	1430.00
Kenya	70	131	172	295	201	869.00
Madagascar	—	60	301	—	3	364.00
Malawi	45	60	140	70	131	446.00
Mali	—	—	40	149	—	189.00
Mauritania	—	16	62	65	5	148.00
Mauritius	15	40	25	—	—	80.00
Mozambique	—	—	89	90	180	359.00
Niger	—	—	140	—	—	140.00
Nigeria	—	250	452	620	—	1322.00
Rwanda	—	—	—	90	—	90.00
São Tomé e P.	—	—	197	10	—	207.00
Senegal	60	—	149	125	5	339.00

Table A5.1 (*Continued*)

Country	1980–82	1983–85	1986–88	1989–91	1992–93	Total
Sierra Leone	—	22	—	—	44	66.00
Somalia	—	—	63	70	—	133.00
Sudan	65	50	—	—	—	115.00
Tanzania	50	—	96	335	223	704.00
Togo	—	78	45	69	—	192.00
Uganda	—	70	65	225	228	588.00
Zaïre	—	—	229	—	—	229.00
Zambia	—	110	118	237	131	596.00
Zimbabwe	—	71	—	—	300	371.00

Source: World Bank, 1992a, 1992b, 1993c

Notes

1 A recent application of the two-gap model can be found in Lensink (1993)
2 See the appendix to Chapter 2 (*cf.* equations A7a and A7b).
3 I ignore any possible changes in international reserves
4 RMSM-X is an extension of the RMSM with additional aspects taken from the IMF model on financial programmes. The number of sectors is increased substantially and the RMSM-X pays far more attention to monetary variables. The RMSM-XX models represent the most recent generation of macroeconomic World Bank models. These are RMSM-X models extended with behavioural equations for the most important macroeconomic variables. Unlike the RMSM and RMSM-X models, the RMSM-XX is a macroeconometric model which is solved simultaneously. The World Bank objective is to extend the RMSM-XX to a standard macroeconometric model in which advanced behavioural equations are implemented in a basic system of national accounts, i.e. the MACOR model.

Examples of World Bank activities concerning models can be found in Bruce and Ndii (1991), Easterly (1989), Easterly *et al.* (1990), Elbadawi and Majd (1993), Elbadawi and Schmidt-Hebbel (1991), Everaert *et al.* (1990), Khadr and Schmidt-Hebbel (1989), and Serven (1990).

6 Structural adjus programmes by and the World Ba

In this chapter I shall describe in detail the structural adjustment programmes which have been implemented with the help of the IMF and the World Bank.[1] Section 6.1 describes how the relation between the IMF and the World Bank developed during the past decades. Section 6.2 presents an introduction to the conditions as presented in the adjustment programmes. Since devaluation is quite essential in the adjustment programmes, the African exchange rate policy will feature in Section 6.3. Section 6.4 will present a survey of the main elements of adjustment programmes; with respect to the significance of the measures concerning trade, agriculture and the government respectively, Sections 6.5, 6.6 and 6.7 will deal with these specific issues; Section 6.8 will discuss some other components of the adjustment programmes. Finally, Section 6.9 will offer a summary of this chapter.

6.1 The relation between the World Bank and the IMF

Until the 1980s there was a clear distinction between the World Bank and the IMF. The World Bank mandate referred to promoting economic recovery and development, while the task of the IMF was to promote international monetary cooperation. The IMF aimed at the short term and was strongly oriented towards the demand side of the economy, while the World Bank was more directed towards the long term and mainly concentrated on the supply side of the economy. The IMF loans were programme loans to finance balance of payments deficits; World Bank loans mainly referred to supporting projects, that is project lending. In Table 6.1 the traditional differences between the IMF and the World Bank are contrasted.

The relation between the IMF and the World Bank changed in the course of time, and the spheres of activity of the two institutions are now overlapping. Programme lending, which was the exclusive right of the IMF, became an important aspect of World Bank credit facilities when the SALs and SECALs were introduced. The IMF started to concentrate more on the medium and long term as far as the additional credit facilities (EFF, SAF and ESAF) were concerned. The stabilisation programmes aim at the short term, but by introducing the extended fund facility (EFF) the IMF

… elation of IMF and World Bank

	IMF	World Bank
…haracter	monetary institution	developmental institution
aim	monetary stability	promotion of economic development
	financing temporary deficits in the balance of payments	financing economic development
term	short term	long term
orientation	demand side of the economy	supply side of the economy
credit	to all member states	to developing countries
	programme lending	project lending

Sources: Bakker, 1992, p. 66; Bird, 1993

officially acknowledged the significance of a policy directed towards the medium term. The IMF felt that a policy exclusively aimed at stabilisation could not solve the problems concerning the balance of payments of developing countries, at most it could relieve them temporarily. Introducing the concessional structural adjustment facilities was eventually the result of this line of reasoning. The scope of both the IMF and the World Bank increasingly includes accommodating programme loans, conditional on policy changes; the two institutions are also involved in adjustment programmes in the countries that are granted loans. This is confirmed by the fact that the IMF primarily lent money to developing countries during the 1980s (Bird, 1993).

The great overlap which currently exists with respect to IMF and World Bank activities results in a number of problems. IMF conditions are quantitive and concrete and refer to existing macroeconomic indicators; non-compliance with the conditions will lead to discontinuation of granting credit. The World Bank, on the other hand, employs not only quantitive conditions in its programmes but often qualitative conditions too. This causes difficulties in determining the achievements of a member state. The Bank is less strict in its granting of credit than the IMF. Differences in the nature of the conditions and in the consequences of not complying with the conditions are confusing to member states who follow programmes of both the IMF and the World Bank.

The objectives of traditional IMF stabilisation programmes and World Bank adjustment programmes do not always match. This results in inconsistencies in the various conditions a member state must comply with. Although it is theoretically possible to distinguish stabilisation from structural adjustment, in practice this distinction is often rather vague. Programmes overlap, and sometimes the precise scope of a programme is not clear.

After the introduction of concessional SAF and ESAF arrangements by the IMF it was absolutely necessary to prevent any inconsistency between conditions by means of proper coordination. The policy framework paper (PFP) was more or less a logical result. These papers, however, cannot absolutely preclude possible inconsistencies between conditions.

The IMF and the World Bank increasingly try to coordinate their policy. At present it is hard to distinguish IMF policies from World Bank policies on Africa. The policy conditions as dictated by the two institutions are identical to a large extent. Taylor (1993) calls this phenomenon 'the Washington consensus'. Still, the desirability of this development may be questioned. Many authors point out the inefficiency of having two international financial institutions operating in the same field. Reconsidering IMF and World Bank tasks, therefore, seems to be highly significant. Bird (1993) argues in favour of giving the World Bank the exclusive right to work with structural adjustment programmes. The IMF should refrain from policy-based lending and it should restrict itself to the traditional task of regulating international financial transactions.[2]

6.2 An introduction to the conditions attached to adjustment lending

In practice, a developing country will turn to the IMF first for a stand-by arrangement in which the IMF will provide financial means to support the measures that are considered to be necessary for short-term repairing of imbalances in the balance of payments and the related government deficits. After the economy has been stabilised, the country will apply for adjustment loans with the World Bank and the IMF. Note that structural adjustment loans often contain stabilisation measures as well.

The official formulation of the structural adjustment programme is the PFP. In principle, the country itself will suggest a description of the fields in which policy changes are required; the World Bank and the IMF will respond to this on the basis of their own diagnosis. Eventually, there will be a suggestion for policy adjustments to which the SAL, SECAL, SAF or ESAF is attached. When the member state accepts this suggestion, the granting of credit can be started. In principle, future granting of credit depends on the degree to which the member state complies with the determined conditions.

The World Bank and the IMF consider devaluation to be crucial to the success of a reform policy. Since in most cases exchange rates are within the scope of the IMF, measures concerning exchange rates are increasingly included in stabilisation programmes and less in structural adjustment programmes. However, new loans are almost always related to a devaluation of the currency since countries cannot acquire structural adjustment loans until they have implemented a stabilisation programme – as has been mentioned above. An exception to this are the programmes for countries in the CFA (African Financial Community) zone (see Section 6.3). Until early 1994, these countries were hardly ever faced with conditions concerning a devaluation of their currencies.[3]

With reference to the great importance of exchange rates – read devaluations – as an instrument in stabilisation programmes that need to be executed before a structural adjustment programme may be entered into, I shall discuss African exchange rate policies and exchange rate systems in closer detail in the next section.

6.3 African exchange rate policies

I shall commence this discussion by introducing several notions that are relevant to this topic.

Exchange rate concepts

Exchange rates reflect the ratio of the currency units of two different countries. The exchange rate may be described in two different ways. The most common notion is the nominal exchange rate. In general, and therefore also in this book, the nominal exchange rate equals the price of the foreign currency expressed in the domestic currency, that is the amount of currency units that has to be paid for one foreign currency unit. In this context, an increase in the exchange rate means a depreciation of the domestic currency.[4]

Another frequently used notion is the real exchange rate. The real exchange rate is the nominal exchange rate after correcting for price differences at home and abroad.[5] The real exchange rate measures the degree to which a country is able to compete with other countries. A real depreciation of the currency means that a country has become cheaper in comparison with foreign countries. This may be a result of a nominal depreciation of the currency, a decrease in domestic prices, or an increase in foreign prices. The real exchange rate is sometimes described as the price of tradable products compared to the price of non-tradable products. The tradable products refer to exports and imports and to products that are not traded but that could be traded. Non-tradable goods are goods such as services (hairdressers, shoeshiners, etc.) that cannot be traded. Thus measured, a real depreciation of the currency is a nominal depreciation of the currency or a decrease in the price of tradable goods expressed in domestic currency as compared with the price of non-tradable goods expressed in the domestic currency.

The so-called real effective exchange rate takes into account the fact that a country has commercial ties with different countries. The effective exchange rate is a weighted average of the (bilateral) exchange rates between the homeland and its trading partners. The 'volume' of the commercial ties of the different trading partners with the homeland is generally used as the weight.

In the debate on the exchange rate policy to be pursued, the real equilibrium exchange rate is often applied. This is the value of the real exchange rate which – given certain long-term values of international prices, foreign commercial capital flows, development aid, and technology – causes both an equilibrium in the balance of payments and an equilibrium on the domestic market. In other words, the real equilibrium exchange rate is the value of the exchange rate where an equilibrium is realised in the balance of payments, provided that the 'sustained' level of foreign capital flows is taken into account. Due to the fact that the long-term values of the above mentioned variables are unknown, it is hard to determine the precise value of the real equilibrium exchange rate.

In relation to the real equilibrium exchange rate, overvalued and undervalued currencies are often mentioned. An overvalued currency has got a value higher than its real equilibrium exchange rate. An overvalued currency causes a deficit in the balance of payments at the sustained level of foreign capital inflows. Theoretically, overvaluation of the currency may have various causes. The IMF mainly points to the consequences of too expansive a monetary and fiscal government policy which stimulates domestic demand. An increase in domestic demand leads to an increase in domestic prices which harms exports and promotes imports. According to the IMF and the World Bank, an overvalued currency not only harms the trade balance, but also promotes capital flight since an overvalued exchange rate raises expectations of a future devaluation. Investors who wish to outstrip this future devaluation of the currency will take their funds abroad (see also Ch. 3).

Exchange rate policies in Africa

One can distinguish different exchange rate systems. The most extreme forms are flexible exchange rates – the exchange rate is entirely determined by demand and supply of a currency, and the central bank does not intervene – and fixed exchange rates – one currency is linked to another currency or a basket of currencies (e.g. SDRs) by means of interventions by the central bank. In practice, most countries have an exchange rate system which is a mixture of these extremes. Often a country has a system of neither fixed nor flexible exchange rates, and its exchange rates are adjusted regularly.

When being granted independence, most African countries knew a system of fixed exchange rates *vis-à-vis* the British pound sterling or the French franc. The pound sterling zone was abolished after some time. The franc zone, however, is currently one of the largest currency blocs in developing countries. The franc zone refers to certain countries divided among two monetary unions: the West African Monetary Union (the WAMU or UMOA) and the Central African Zone (BEAC). The WAMU comprises Benin, Burkina Faso, the Ivory Coast, Mali, Niger, Senegal and Togo; the BEAC consists of Cameroon, the Central African Republic, Chad, the Congo, Equatorial Guinea and Gabon. The Comoros are also part of the franc zone although they are not attached to one of these two monetary unions. The importance of the franc zone to Africa is obvious: the total area of the franc zone includes about 30 per cent of Africa, and GDP in this region amounts to about 20 per cent of the African GDP.

Both monetary unions plus the Comoros have their own central bank and their own currency: the CFA franc, the value of which may differ in the various countries. The central banks of the unions and the Comoros hold an account with the French central bank in which they keep 65 per cent of their foreign reserves in French francs. The French government guarantees the convertibility of the CFA franc. The member states of the franc zone have an open international capital market with free capital flows between members, and France.

In practice, the regional central banks within the CFA zone draw up annual credit intentions for each individual country in order to discourage an overexpansive credit policy. Thus, the credibility of the fixed exchange rate in relation to the French franc is guaranteed. The slight volume of capital flows between members of the monetary unions makes it possible for each member state to formulate independent credit intentions. The credit programmes include target figures for the amount of domestic credit to the public and the private sector. Countries will try to realise their objectives using such instruments as limits to credit banks may grant each other, interest rate policies, and quotas for the amount of credit private banks and the government can contract with the central bank. For example, it has been decided that the government in a member state is not allowed to borrow over 20 per cent of its tax revenues of the previous year from the central bank (IMF Survey, 24 January 1994). The sum of the different plans makes the monetary plan of the entire union.[6]

Numerous studies analyse the pros and cons of the franc zone in relation to other exchange rate systems.[7] An often mentioned advantage is the relatively low inflation resulting from the necessary (in principle, that is) linking of the monetary policy to France's monetary policy. This argument is illustrated in Table 6.2: in the 1980s average inflation in Burkina Faso, Cameroon and the Ivory Coast was far lower than the regional average. Therefore, the franc zone is frequently described as an island of stable prices on the African continent. A disadvantage is the fact that countries that are part of the franc zone cannot use their exchange rates to promote production. By means of devaluation, the negative effects of a deterioration of the terms of trade, for example, may be restricted.

Table 6.2 Exchange rate system and inflation

	Exchange rate system	Inflation 1970–80	Inflation 1980–92
Africa	—	13.6	15.6
East Asia	—	16.6	6.7
South Asia	—	9.7	8.5
Latin America	—	46.7	229.5
Burkina Faso	franc zone	8.6	3.5
Cameroon	franc zone	9.8	3.5
Ghana	flexible	35.2	38.7
Ivory Coast	franc zone	13.0	1.9
Kenya	fixed	10.1	9.3
Madagascar	flexible	9.9	16.4
Nigeria	flexible	15.2	19.4
Tanzania	fixed	14.1	25.3

Sources: Guillaumont and Guillaumont, 1991; World Bank, 1994b

Notes: 'Flexible' refers to limited flexibility. Until 1973 Madagascar was part of the franc zone, after 1973 the currency was linked to the French franc until 1982. Since 1982 there has been a system of more or less flexible exchange rates.

An important subject for debate is the fact whether or not the CFA franc is overvalued in relation to the French franc. Since the establishment of the franc zone until 12 January 1994, 1 French franc buys 50 CFA francs. During the 1980s monetary policy in the franc zone was too expansive, according to the IMF. This was reflected by the accumulation of debt to the central bank of France. Much-needed adjustments of the monetary policy were not carried out, so that the IMF felt that a devaluation of the CFA franc was required. The African countries showed reluctance towards a devaluation because they feared that the people might rebel against the inevitable increase in prices of food and fuel. Moreover, they pointed out the fact that profits by foreign entrepreneurs, expressed in foreign currencies, would fall strongly in CFA countries and that the debt burden would increase sharply. However, on 12 January 1994 the CFA franc devalued for the first time and to an extremely large degree. This devaluation was forced by the IMF who made new loans and debt arrangements dependent on the devaluation. France also played an important role: its future aid would depend on an agreement between the CFA countries and the IMF. The new ratio of values is as follows: 100 CFA francs from the WAMU and the BEAC will buy 1 French franc, and 75 Comoros francs will buy 1 French franc. These devaluations have had serious economic and social consequences. In several CFA countries riots broke out because domestic prices of various basic facilities increased sharply.[8] As a 'reward' for the enforced devaluation, France acquitted the complete debt of the ten poorest countries and 50 per cent of the debts of the four richest countries (Congo, Gabon, the Ivory Coast and Cameroon). The IMF decided to accommodate Senegal and the Ivory Coast with new loans. Time will tell whether the recent devaluations have had the desired positive effects.

In the rest of Africa different exchange rate systems can be identified. The system that is most like the franc zone is the rand zone, comprising South Africa, Lesotho and Swaziland. Here, too, capital flows may flow freely within the zone. Each participating country, however, has its own currency and central bank, so that in principle an independent monetary policy may be pursued. In practice, monetary policies are very much determined by South Africa. The currencies of the different countries in the rand zone are convertible in the proportion of 1 to 1.

Unlike the franc and rand zones, the rest of Africa is faced with substantial restrictions in the international currency market (Devarajan and Rodrik, 1992). In some countries the currency is linked to the dollar (e.g. in Ethiopia, Mozambique, Somalia, the Sudan, Uganda and Zambia); in other countries it is linked to the SDR (for example, in Kenya, Rwanda and Burundi). In these countries the government determines the exchange rates. The sale of foreign currencies is usually conducted by the government; the government also decides who may use the foreign currencies.

The devaluations that are implemented from time to time in a system of fixed yet adjustable exchange rates are to make sure that the official exchange rate does not deviate too much from the market exchange rate, that is the exchange rate that would apply if there had been a system of freely floating exchange rates. In some countries the difference between the official exchange rate and the market exchange rate, the misalignment, could be restricted by means of officially implemented devaluations. In the majority of African countries devaluations have been too small. The actual value of the domestic currency became much lower than its official value, so that a black market came into being on which the domestic currency was traded at a lower value for hard foreign currencies. This led to a situation in which a considerable part of currency trade took place on the black market so that capital controls could be avoided. In extreme situations, like in Ghana in the early 1980s, the official exchange rate was no longer relevant to the market. In such cases exchange rates are only used as a monetary unit for government transactions. The exchange rate on the black market determines the real price of foreign currencies, so that prices of tradable goods are determined to a large extent by the black market exchange rate.[9] Table 6.3 presents the percentage difference between the exchange rate on the black market and the official exchange rate (expressed in the domestic currency) for a number of African countries.

The World Bank and the IMF emphasise the negative effects of the African exchange rates which they consider to be overvalued. This overvaluation is partly reflected by the above presented difference between the official exchange rate and the exchange rate on the black market. The overvalued exchange rate not only affects unfavourably exports, but also is conducive to smuggling. Many exporters decide to smuggle their own products out of the country so that their products will fetch more money than they would if the exporter had gone through the official channels. Thus, the amount of foreign currency transferred to the government for importing essential means of production decreases.

An understanding of the process of overvaluation is also provided by considering the real effective exchange rate. In Table 6.4, in contrast to usual practice, an increase in the real exchange rate implies that competitiveness has improved. The table shows that for most African countries competitiveness improved during the 1980s. Ghana, Nigeria and Tanzania experienced a substantial real appreciation during the early 1980s after which they saw a considerable real depreciation. Since the value of the equilibrium exchange rate is unknown, it remains unclear whether exchange rates have been sufficiently adjusted. According to the IMF and the World Bank, currencies are still overvalued in most countries. For the early 1980s this notion is confirmed in a study by Dollar (1992) who tries to calculate the degree of overvaluation. The figures in his study refer to an average of the 1976–85 period. The study shows that

Table 6.3 The premium on exchange rates on the black market

	1981–86	1990	1993
Ghana	1098.2	7.3	1.4
Kenya	15.2	5.9	32.0
Madagascar	42.0	7.1	9.5
Nigeria	237.7	23.4	128.5
Tanzania	248.8	78.0	1.7

Sources: Bouton *et al*., 1994, Table B8; World Bank, 1994a, Table A.5

Note: Premium = (Black market rate minus the official rate)/Official rate

Table 6.4 real effective exchange rate (1980 = 100)

	1981	1985	1990	1992
Ghana	45	190	480	518
Ivory Coast	119	138	96	94
Kenya	104	100	143	140
Madagascar	95	109	193	208
Nigeria	90	59	352	504
Tanzania	77	49	272	299

Source: Bouton *et al.*, 1994

especially in Ghana, Nigeria and Tanzania overvaluation has been extremely significant in this period.

6.4 A survey of the conditions in structural adjustment programmes

The conditions the World Bank and the IMF attach to the granting of credit refer to improving investment and entrepreneurial climate, markets for production factors, and management of means in the public sector, and reforms of social policies (World Bank, 1992a). Table 6.5 presents the relative importance of the conditions in these fields to Africa, as well as the percentage of loans these conditions refer to. The table shows that most conditions apply to trade policies, agricultural policies, and the improvement of management of the public sector. In the sections below I shall discuss these three important aspects of adjustment programmes in detail.

6.5 Trade policy

One of the main items of adjustment policies is trade policy. In 1989 this was actually the area that most conditions had been attached to (Greenaway and Morrissey, 1993, p. 243). Table 6.6 presents the share of conditions relevant to trade policy and exchange rates in the total number of conditions for Africa, in comparison to other developing countries in the course of time. Conditions relating to reforms of exchange rate systems will also be discussed here since the exchange rate policy affects trade directly and significantly.

Table 6.6 shows that the total number of conditions relating to trade policy is high for Africa during the 1980–92 period, although it is lower than for the other countries. Moreover, the share of the conditions relating to trade policies decreased during the past few years. The aim of the adjustments of the trade policy is to diminish the disadvantage of the commercial sector, particularly the export sector. The measures consist of reforms of the import and export sector.

Table 6.5 Conditions attached to adjustment loans 1989–91

	Relative importance	at % of loans
improving investment and entrepr. climate	31	
exchange rate policy	2	14
trade policy	9	52
monetary policy	1	14
industrial policy	1	12
energy policy	2	12
agricultural policy	12	40
other sectors	4	14
improving factor markets	8	
financial sector	4	24
incomes policy	4	31
improving management public sector	48	
expenditure policy	16	81
rationalisation public expenditure and apparatus of government	17	90
public enterprise reforms	15	67
reforms of social policy	10	24
remaining	5	

Source: World Bank, 1992a

Note: The second column shows the percentage of conditions attached to particular policies in relation to the total number of conditions attached to adjustment loans, so that it shows the relative importance of a certain type of policy. The third column shows the percentage of loans with conditions attached to the policies indicated.

Import reforms refer to three aspects (World Bank, 1994a):

- distribution of foreign currency for importing goods and services
- elimination of non-tariff-related restrictions
- reforms of tariffs.

Distribution of foreign currency for importing goods and services

In most African countries exporters and importers can dispose of foreign currency only within certain boundaries. Often exporters have to 'sell' their earned foreign

Table 6.6 Significance of conditions referring to trade policy and exchange rates (% of total or % of conditions attached to trade policy)

	Africa	Other	ITS	QRXM	ER
1980	40	29	20	20	10
1983	17	27	11	7	21
1986	19	24	9	18	18
1989	12	18	33	14	23
1990	6	10	11	20	14
1991	11	13	27	25	9
1992	10	11	17	26	16
1980–92	12	17	22	17	17

Source: Nash, 1993, Tables 1 and 2

Notes: 'Other' refers to countries outside Africa; ITS = import tariffs and subsidies; QRXM = quantitive restrictions on exports and imports; ER = exchange rates. ITS, QRXM and ER are expressed in percentages of the total number of conditions referring to trade and exchange rates.

currency within a certain period to the government at the official – and usually overvalued – exchange rate. Since the foreign currency has to be sold to the government at the overvalued, official exchange rate, the exporters receive less domestic currency than they would have if they had exchanged the foreign currency at the equilibrium exchange rate (in accordance with the exchange rate on the black market). The government, moreover, decides by means of import licences who may use the foreign currency to import the goods selected by the government. If the importer is granted an import licence, the importer can take this licence to the central bank and buy the required amount of foreign currency. Thus the government can protect the domestic industrial sector. After all, the government may not grant import licences to imports that compete with goods that are also produced at home. However, this system does encourage importers to purchase the required foreign currency on the black market. An exporter who is forced to transfer the foreign currency earned at the overvalued official exchange rate and may buy the required foreign currency for imports on the black market – where a greater amount of domestic currency has to be paid for the foreign currency – in fact pays taxes on exports which will equal the difference between the value of the currency on the black market and at the official exchange rate. Even when the exporter does not do business on the black market and when the distribution system functions properly, the exporter is faced with additional costs. For the exporter receives the 'demand price' for the foreign currency earned through exports, but the exporter will have to pay the 'supply price' to obtain the foreign currency required for imports. The World Bank and the IMF, therefore, state that this complex system of distribution hampers exports and stimulates inefficient domestic production. The hindering of the export sector leads to a shift from production aimed at exports to production for the domestic market, which highly reduces opportunities to earn foreign currencies. Consequently, the required imports can no longer be paid for, and this will result in stagnating production, a shortage of certain products, and high prices for consumer goods.

The structural adjustment programmes contain measures to reform the system of distributing foreign currencies, for example the exchange auctions in, for instance, Ghana, Nigeria, Uganda, Zambia and Guinea. Importers can obtain international currencies at an auction rather than by means of licences. At an exchange auction the available amount of foreign currency is distributed by the central bank by means of an auction. Potential buyers bid for the foreign currency, indicating how much of the foreign currency they wish to buy and at what price. The central bank subsequently distributes the available amount of foreign currency. At a Dutch auction all participants pay the price of their own bid. In such a system different prices are paid for the same product (read foreign currency). In a system of marginal prices everyone will pay the equilibrium price, which corresponds with the lowest bid. The Dutch auction system can be found in Nigeria, Uganda, Zambia and Ghana. Guinea applies the 'marginal price system' (La Ferrara *et al.*, 1994). It is often argued that the Dutch exchange auctions are a beginning of attempts to liberalise the international currency market. The 'marginal price system' is comparable to a completely free market. The selection of products that can be bought with the foreign currency acquired at exchange auctions ought to be increased in the course of time.

Another element of the reforms is legalising the use of the international currency earned by exporters, that is export proceeds retention schemes. Exporters are allowed to keep part of the foreign currency they have earned. The rest has to be 'sold' to the government at the official exchange rate. The currencies that are not sold may be used for importing products selected by the government. The good thing about this is that exporters are not faced with a difference between the demand and supply price of the foreign currency. The export proceeds retention schemes especially apply to the large non-traditional exporters. The traditional (coffee, cocoa, etc.) and small exporters are usually not granted the opportunity to use these schemes. The absolute majority of total exports consists of traditional exports. The export retention schemes, therefore, apply only to a small part of exports.

Another example of the legalisation of foreign currencies are the own-funds systems (for example, in Tanzania and Zambia). Each individual who owns foreign currency – irrespective of how they obtained it – may use the currency to import a selection of goods. The goods may be imported without restrictions as long as the official foreign reserves are not used. The drawback of this system is that trading on the black market to buy foreign currencies is encouraged, so that the difference between the official exchange rate and the rate on the black market grows.

Liberalisation of the distribution of foreign currency is also promoted by developing private financial institutions that are in charge of selling and buying foreign currency – at a price fixed by these same institutions. Often this actually amounts to legalising the existing exchange offices on the black market. Thus, attempts are made at controlling part of the informal black market and reducing the difference between the official rate and the rate on the black market.

Elimination of non-tariff-related restrictions

The adjustment programmes incorporate measures to limit non-tariff-related restrictions. This partly amounts to reforming the distribution of international currencies (see the above discussion). Other reforms especially refer to the system of licences where the number of imports that required licences was sharply reduced. Open general licensing systems or liberalised import regimes are introduced. In such systems several goods are selected for which import licences and foreign currencies – at a subsidised exchange rate – are automatically made available. The order of liberalisations is usually as follows (La Ferrera *et al.*, 1994, p. 8): during the initial phase a list of goods that may be imported is drawn up. Usually these imports are essential production factors only. As time goes by, the list of authorised imports is replaced with a list of goods that may not be imported. By now the selection of authorised imports has been highly expanded.

A much applied protectionist measure in Africa is the condition that forces importers to deposit the exchange for the required amount of foreign currency with the central bank or the government well in advance. This condition functions rather like an import tariff since it increases the costs of imports due to the loss of interest revenues on the deposit. Several adjustment programmes have decided to abolish this protectionist measure.

Reform of tariffs

The principal element of the conditions of trade policies is reforming the system of import tariffs. The present standard recommendation refers to raising the tariffs on final goods after abolishing the non-tariff-related restrictions, and to gradually reform tariffs. Most African countries use a complex system of import tariffs with tariffs differing for each product. An important element of tariff reforms, therefore, is reducing the variety of tariffs. In connection with this, the difference between the highest and the lowest tariffs is reduced in many adjustment programmes. Eventually, the actual tariffs are lowered. With reference to the great importance of the revenues from tariffs as a source of income for the government, as yet most African countries have not succeeded in reducing tariffs substantially. However, there are indeed some deviations from this standard pattern. For example, in Kenya and Ghana tariff reductions were preceded by the limiting of non-tariff-related restrictions.

Apart from import reforms, trade policies consist of promoting exports. Liberalisation of the distribution of foreign currencies is but one example; devaluations of the currency, reduction of taxes on exports, regulations relating to exporting activities, and reforming the marketing organisations that are in charge of exporting goods are some other examples. In some countries (Nigeria, Tanzania and Uganda) several exporters were offered the opportunity to use a more devaluated currency. In other countries (for example, in Kenya and Nigeria) free trade zones were established where exporters were exempt from taxes on imported inputs and exports. In several adjustment programmes restrictive measures concerning foreign investment were reduced.

6.6 Agricultural policy[10]

Another type of policy adjustment programmes is directed towards agricultural policy. Measures to stimulate agricultural production, in fact, refer to decreasing the traditional disadvantage of the agricultural sector. Devaluation of the currency is an important instrument since the agricultural sector was the traditional export sector. Moreover, taxes on exports are reduced. Many conditions refer to reforming the marketing organisations (see Ch. 3). The World Bank points out the inefficiency of these organisations and argues that discontinuance or privatisation is necessary.

Reforms of the marketing organisations can be divided into three categories (World Bank, 1994a, p. 81):

- discontinuance of marketing organisations
- reform of marketing organisations
- authorising the existence of private organisations as well as marketing organisations.

Discontinuance of marketing organisations

In some countries, like Nigeria, all marketing organisations have been discontinued. In most countries only marketing organisations for certain products have been abolished (e.g. in Madagascar for peanuts).

Reform of marketing organisations

The marketing organisations continue to exist but reforms are being implemented. The aim of these reforms is to reduce the costs of the organisations. One also tries to improve the consistency of producer prices and prices on the world market. For example, West and Central Africa experiment with a system where cotton producers receive the proceeds from their products in two separate stages. During the first stage, the marketing organisation, in charge of exports, pays a fixed amount for the products to the producers. Next, a variable amount, depending on the profits of the marketing organisations, is paid to the producers. Thus, producers cannot immediately use the difference between export prices and the anticipated price, which has been fixed by the marketing organisation.

Authorising the existence of private organisations as well as marketing organisations

In many adjustment programmes the private sector is encouraged to develop competitive organisations so that the monopoly of the state-led marketing organisations is affected. In some countries (e.g. in the Ivory Coast for coffee and cocoa) the private sector was allowed to compete with the marketing organisations with regard to the domestic purchasing policy. Government control over exports was maintained, though.

An important element of agricultural policy refers to distributing and subsidising fertilisers. In Africa fertilisers are not used on that large a scale. According to the World Bank, this is due to the scarcity of fertiliser and the inadequate distribution entailed by numerous government regulations. According to the World Bank, subsidies for fertilisers should be abolished since – with the given shortage of finance – these subsidies will reduce the supply of fertiliser. The money would be better spent on activities that increase the profitability of the agricultural sector, like rural infrastructure or agricultural research. Distribution of fertiliser – which is done through the government channels and considered to be rather inefficient by the World Bank – should be liberalised.

6.7 Management of the public sector

The adjustment programmes refer to a large extent to the restructuring of the public sector. The World Bank and the IMF place great emphasis on the far too extensive apparatus of government in most African countries, which they consider to be functioning inefficiently. Improving management in the public sector refers to pushing down government deficits – which is also a crucial requirement in IMF stabilisation programmes (see Ch. 4) – reforming the tax system and the civil service, abolishing subsidies, and reforming or privatising public enterprises.

Often the first step is to draw up a list of existing public enterprises. Strategic and non-strategic enterprises arc distinguished. The non-strategic enterprises are divided into viable and unviable enterprises. The viable non-strategic enterprises are often privatised. The unviable public enterprises, that are of no strategic importance, are liquidated. A total of about 550 relatively small enterprises – less than one-fifth of the total number of public enterprises in Africa – have been either privatised or liquidated. Note that two-thirds of all privatisations and liquidations took place in Benin, Ghana, Guinea, Mozambique, Nigeria and Senegal (World Bank, 1994a, p. 104). The strategic public enterprises, such as transport, telecommunications, heavy industry, and agricultural marketing organisations, usually stay under government management. In general, restructuring happens by means of developing certain objectives the enterprises must try to realise.

Government budget deficits have to be lowered. Reducing subsidies and the number of civil servants will cause a reduction in spending. A reduction in the number of civil servants is realised by introducing a compulsory pensionable age, abolishing the guaranteeing of government positions for people with a university education, and firing superfluous civil servants. By means of commercialising public services, like introducing reimbursements of expenses for education received, and reforming the tax system, revenues will be increased.

6.8 Remaining measures in adjustment programmes

The adjustment programmes also refer to the financial sector, and in particular to the banking sector.[11] The regular objective is to realise a positive real interest. To this end, interest ceilings are abolished, and state-led granting of credit to certain sectors is reduced. In several countries the interest rates are completely liberalised (Gambia, Ghana, Kenya, Madagascar, Mauritania and Zambia). Furthermore, credit facilities and banks managed by the government are restructured. In many African countries the banking sector is dominated by the government. It is only in a few countries (e.g. the Ivory Coast, Kenya, Nigeria and Zambia) that there are several private banks that are not controlled by the government to a large extent. In many cases a new government organisation is established which takes over the 'bad' loans. Moreover, banks receive capital injections which enable them to make a new start with respect to their financing tasks. In Guinea-Bissau, Madagascar and Senegal, part of the restructured banks was privatised. In Ghana and Tanzania the restructured banks remained under government management. Some credit facilities were abolished. Developing training programmes for banking personnel, changing regulations, and improving supervision of banks must lead to a better financial infrastructure.

Some adjustment programmes attach conditions to monetary policy to reduce monetary financing. A tight monetary policy is striven for. Government credit by the central bank should be restricted (see also Ch. 4).

Conditions are also attached to the industrial and the energy sector. Again the objective is to improve the investment and entrepreneurial climate by reforming regulations and abolishing price monitoring. Privatisation is the key word in World Bank and IMF policies referring to the industrial sector.

The adjustment programmes further consist of conditions with regard to income policy. All sorts of regulations on the labour market ought to be abolished in order to improve labour mobility. A reduction of wage indexing to price movements is an important condition in this respect.

Finally, there are conditions that refer to social policy. The aim of these measures is to improve health care and education and to protect the poor during the period of adjustment.[12]

6.9 Summary

In the course of time the World Bank and the IMF have moved into each other's fields of activity. Both the IMF and the World Bank accommodate programme lending to countries that are prepared to implement a structural adjustment programme. Moreover, both institutions are involved in structural adjustment programmes in the same countries, and PFPs, in which the programmes are described, are written by the World Bank in association with the IMF. It is quite difficult, therefore, to distinguish World Bank policies from IMF policies on Africa.

Adjustment programmes are mainly inspired by neoclassical theory. The World

Bank and the IMF start from the notion that opening up the economy and letting markets work with realistic prices provide the best opportunity for economic development. The principal aspects of adjustment programmes refer to international trade, the agricultural sector and the government. Attempts are made at reducing the traditional disadvantage of the foreign trade sector. Important measures in this area are devaluation of the currency and reforming tariff-related and non-tariff-related restrictions. The measures that refer to the agricultural sector aim at stimulating agricultural production. The conditions especially relate to reforming marketing organisations. Finally, the inefficient public sector is one of the main causes of the present crisis in Africa, according to the World Bank and IMF. Therefore, the adjustment programmes include conditions which have to result in a reduction of the number of civil servants and the privatisation of public enterprises.

Notes

1 This chapter draws from Lensink and Vijselaar (1995).

2 For a debate on the future of the two Bretton Woods institutions see also the various articles in International Economic Insights (Institute for International Economics, 1993) and the articles in Bretton Woods Commission (1994).

3 In several countries in the CFA zone – especially Senegal and the Ivory Coast – subsidies for certain exports were introduced. At the same time import tariffs were raised with a view to imitating devaluations, so-called mock devaluations.

4 Sometimes the nominal exchange rate is described as the price of the domestic currency expressed in the foreign currency, i.e. the amount of foreign currency units that has to be paid for one domestic currency unit. In that case an increase in the exchange rate is an appreciation.

5 Contrary to the way in which the nominal exchange rate is defined, in most studies an increase in the real exchange rate is a real appreciation of the domestic currency.

6 For a description of the functioning of the franc zone, see Honohan (1990a; 1990b).

7 For some detailed analyses of the pros and cons of the franc zone I refer to Chhibber (1992), Claassen (1992), Devarajan and de Melo (1991), Devarajan and Rodrik (1992) and Guillamont and Guillamont (1991).

8 For example, in Congo the price of medications doubled, and in the Ivory Coast the price of bread increased by 50 per cent.

9 Montiel *et al.* (1993) have discussed the pros and cons of the existence of a black market for foreign currencies.

10 In general, the measures concerning agricultural policy are linked to SECALs aimed at the agricultural sector. The World Bank does indeed play a more important part than the IMF.

11 For a discussion on the pros and cons of financial liberalisation see, for example, Fry (1988), Gupta (1984), and Gupta and Lensink (1993).

12 In 1987 the World Bank introduced the Social Dimensions of Adjustment (SDA) which try to improve the social consequences of adjustment programmes. The World Bank contribution to the SDA, however, is rather small as yet. For the 1988–91 period financial support by the World Bank to the SDA was less than 2 per cent of the funds granted through the Bank's structural adjustment facilities (Taube, 1993, p. 169).

7 The economic resu the structural adjus programmes

Having discussed the conditions the IMF and the World Bank attach to the granting of adjustment loans, I shall now consider the effectiveness of these programmes.[1] In this chapter the adjustment programmes of both institutions will be evaluated with regard to their economic effects. Most countries executed IMF and World Bank stabilisation or structural adjustment programmes simultaneously. This makes it difficult to distinguish the separate effects of the programmes of the two institutions. Therefore, the evaluation refers to the joint effects of these programmes.

Evaluating structural adjustment programmes means that the contribution of the programmes to a country's macroeconomic achievements needs to be determined. One ought to consider also other factors that affect these achievements and the question of what the situation would have been like if this country had not implemented a structural adjustment programme. It is not easy to select the perfect procedure for an evaluation. The studies that will be discussed in Section 7.2 have been categorised according to the various methods that have been applied in practice. Attention will also be paid to the problems involved in using these methods. Ample attention will be paid to a World Bank report (1994a), in which it is stated that adjustment programmes in Africa have been very successful; I shall investigate whether this statement is justified. Prior to discussing the methods of evaluation, in Section 7.1 I shall consider whether the policy measures of the IMF and the World Bank have actually been executed by the adjusting countries. It is obvious that the degree to which the policy recommendations by the IMF and the World Bank have been implemented is crucial to the effectiveness and suitability of adjustment programmes. If the macroeconomic development of a country does not improve after having been granted an adjustment loan, this could be the result both of the contents of the adjustment programme and of the degree to which the adjustment programme has been executed. The conclusions in Section 7.3 will complete this chapter.

The degree to which the adjustment programmes have been implemented

The World Bank (1992a) presents a survey of the degree to which the policy conditions have been effectuated. This study indicates for each adjustment region the percentage of the desired adjustments that has been fully executed and the percentage of the adjustments that has been executed for a substantial part. The study comes to the conclusion that the majority of the adjustments called for by the World Bank has been executed. When the programmes end, about three-quarters of the conditions in the adjustment programmes have been executed completely, and almost 19 per cent has been executed for a substantial part. The situation for Africa is hardly different from those in other countries with adjustment programmes if the total of all conditions is considered.

In a study by Nash (1993), the execution of conditions concerning trade and exchange rate policies is pursued in greater depth. Nash's study refers to the 1980–92 period. The study suggests that about 65 per cent of the measures relating to trade and exchange rate policies has been completely executed, 19 per cent substantially, and 16 per cent to a limited extent only. The figures for adjusting countries outside Africa are 55, 19 and 22 respectively. In the African countries which are members of the CFA zone, about 26 per cent of the measures has been executed to a limited extent. Especially in relation to export tariffs, subsidies and the export institutions' execution of measures leaves much to be desired. Africa did execute the measures called for with respect to exchange rate policy, quantitive trade restrictions, and import tariffs and subsidies to a substantial extent.

Both above-mentioned studies suggest that the African countries did execute the desired adjustment programmes to a reasonable extent. Still, some objections must be made concerning this conclusion. Greenaway and Milner (1993, p. 227) point out three problems involved in this type of analysis.

First, it is possible that the least important conditions have been implemented whereas the more important ones have not. It is rather telling that Nash (1993) concludes that in the area of trade and exchange rate policies Africa scored high on small reforms, but that the main conditions were executed to a much more limited extent than in non-African countries. With respect to the principal reforms in trade and exchange rate policies, about 18 per cent of all measures has not been executed in Africa, whereas this percentage was a mere 6.5 per cent in countries outside the African continent. For African countries in the CFA zone the situation is even worse. However, note that Nash's study is not very clear on what exactly the important and less important reforms are.

Second, the analysis does not distinguish between the various countries. It could well be that the execution of the programmes was best in those countries with most favourable economic prospects and that problem countries did not properly execute the measures.

Third, it could be that unsuitable conditions were included in the adjustment programmes. Many economists, in particular the structuralists, doubt the effectiveness of measures relating to trade policy and the advantages of a more liberal trade policy.

From the above analyses no conclusions can be drawn with respect to the effects of the adjustment programmes on macroeconomic development of the countries involved. By analysing the degree to which the programmes were executed, the inputs in the adjustment programmes are considered. However, what is more important are the outputs, the results of the reform process.

7.2 A survey of the studies

Evaluating the effects of the structural adjustment programmes involves many problems. A number of problems depends on the method selected. Whichever method is applied, the actual degree of execution remains unknown: are the disappointing results to be attributed to the poor execution of the programme or to the programme itself? Another problem of practically all methods is that it is not clear how much time has to go by before the adjustments affect macroeconomic development. Many measures in the structural adjustment programmes refer to restructuring the economy, the effects of which will not be noted after a short time. Finally, the indicators which most studies used to evaluate the effects of the adjustment programmes are disputable. Almost all evaluations rely on macroeconomic data for real GDP, savings and investment. However, Gunning (1994) states that it may be more worthwhile to use disaggregated microeconomic indicators to evaluate whether the adjustment programmes have improved the allocation of capital and labour between different sectors. Moreover, Gunning (1994) argues that a decline in one of the above-mentioned indicators does not necessarily imply that the adjustment programme failed. It may simply be the result of an optimal adjustment.

Studies based on the 'before and after' method

The most frequently used method in evaluating adjustment programmes is the 'before and after' method. Especially the IMF and the World Bank apply this particular method. The method is basically a comparison of several macroeconomic variables of a country during the period before and the period after the implementation of the adjustment programme. A specific problem of this method is that it starts from several implicit assumptions. The first one is the assumption that exogenous shocks or measures that are not mentioned in the adjustment programme do not influence the economy. This assumption is certainly not a trivial one. For example, it is *a priori* unclear whether a change in economic growth is the result of an adjustment programme, of a change in the terms of trade, or of an increase in Western demand. The next implicit assumption is that the policy pursued before the introduction of the adjustment programmes would have been continued had the adjustment programme not been developed. This, however, is highly unlikely since the adjustment programmes are often introduced during crises. Therefore, it is quite certain that the country in question would have introduced a policy adjustment without IMF or World Bank interference. The evaluation is furthermore obscured when a country implements several programmes simultaneously. Moreover, the adjustment programmes always involve financial support by the World Bank or the IMF. If the economic growth before and after the introduction of the programmes is compared, it is not clear whether the possibly positive effects are caused by the execution of the measures or by the additional financial means that were made available.

Using the 'before and after' method, the IMF (Schadler *et al.*, 1993) evaluated the effects of the ESAF in nineteen countries that qualified for ESAF funds. The study is very positive about the effects of the adjustment programmes. It concludes that 'While there remains considerable room for improvement, the ESAF countries have on average seen a strengthening in a wide range of macroeconomic indicators' (Schadler *et al.* 1993, p. 39). A detailed consideration of the IMF research, however, shows that a lot can be said against this conclusion. To be sure, progress has been made with respect to the average growth of GDP (9 per cent), exports (1 per cent), inflation (11 per cent), imports (2 per cent), and the average ratio between investment and savings in relation to GDP, but at the same time there are huge differences between countries and many deviations from the average, so that it is almost impossible to get an overall picture of the effects of adjustment programmes. Moreover, the average increase of savings in relation to GDP proves to be rather small.

Studying the averages may leave one with a completely distorted picture, though. Table 7.1, therefore, indicates the percentage of African countries in the IMF study that has made progress with regard to the specific variables. It appears that in over 50 per cent of the cases the growth of exports decreased. This is in sharp contrast with the great improvement of the growth of exports – which is actually implied by the IMF – due to adjustment programmes. Moreover, it turns out that the investment/GDP ratio practically increased as frequently as it decreased. The IMF acknowledges the slight response of investment as a result of the adjustment programmes to be one of the greater disappointments.

The World Bank has analysed the adjustment programmes implemented in Africa (World Bank, 1994a).[2] Characteristic of this study is the fact that countries are divided

Table 7.1 Percentage of countries that show progress: IMF study

	Growth GDP	Growth exports	Growth imports	Inflation	Inv/GDP	Sav/GDP
Group 1	71	43	57	63	57	57
Group 2	50	33	50	71	50	80
Total	62	38	54	67	54	67

Source: Deduced from Schadler *et al.*, 1993, Table 11

Notes: The percentages refer to a comparison of the 'latest three years' with the period before SAF/ESAF. Group 1 refers to the group of African countries that made most progress with respect to their foreign debts. Group 2 refers to the group of African countries that have made least progress with respect to their foreign debts. Total refers to the entire group of African countries. Inv: investment. Sav: savings.

into three groups – with respect to the fiscal policy pursued, the monetary policy pursued, and the exchange rate policy pursued: countries with large positive changes in the economic policy, countries with small positive changes in the economic policy, and countries where the economic policy has deteriorated. In this context the 1981–86 period is compared to the 1987–91 period. Per item a country can score a maximum of plus 3 and a minimum of minus 3 points. The total score is the average of the scores on all three items. A country with a total score higher than 1 is ranked among the countries with a great improvement in their policy; countries that score between 0 and 1 are ranked among the countries with a slight improvement in their economic policy; and the countries with a negative score are ranked among the countries that have a deteriorating economic policy. On the basis of the above the World Bank divides countries as follows:

1 countries with large positive improvements in economic policy: Ghana, Tanzania, the Gambia, Burkina Faso, Nigeria and Zimbabwe
2 countries with small positive changes in economic policy: Madagascar, Malawi, Burundi, Kenya, Mali, Mauritania, Senegal, Niger and Uganda
3 countries with a deterioration in economic policy: Benin, the Central African Republic, Rwanda, Sierra Leone, Togo, Zambia, Mozambique, Congo, the Ivory Coast, Cameroon and Gabon.

Subsequently, each group is studied for any improvement in economic achievement. A summary of this study is presented in Table 7.2, which shows the percentage of countries, per group and for the total of the three groups, that has made progress in agricultural growth (agriculture), industrial growth (industry), the growth of per capita GDP (GDPPC), the growth of exports, investment as a percentage of GDP, and savings as a percentage of GDP. This table also shows whether there has been an improvement (+) or a deterioration (−) of the macroeconomic indicators in the six countries I have selected.

Table 7.2 Percentage of countries that have made progress: World Bank study (1987–91 versus 1981–86)

	Agriculture	Industry	GDPPC	Exports	Inv/GDP	SAV/GDP
Group 1	50	83	66	100	67	83
Group 2	50	71	56	63	78	50
Group 3	45	55	45	40	18	20
Total	48	67	54	59	50	46
Ghana	+	+	+	+	+	+
Ivory Coast	+	−	−	+	−	−
Kenya	−	+	+	+	+	−
Madagascar	+	+	+	+	+	+
Nigeria	+	+	+	+	−	+
Tanzania	+	+	+	N.A.	+	−

Source: Composed from World Bank, 1994a, Tables A.20, A.21, A.22, A.23, A.24 and 5.1

What then can be concluded from Table 7.2? When the total group of countries is considered, the achievements appear to be rather discouraging. In general only 50 per cent of all countries has made progress per distinguished variable. A positive exception is industrial growth: 67 per cent of the countries experienced an increase in the average industrial growth during the 1987–91 period as compared to the 1981–86 period.

A comparison between the various groups shows that in general there is a relation between an improvement in economic policy – as observed by the World Bank – and an improvement in economic achievements. The percentage of countries with an improvement in economic achievements is almost always highest for the group of countries with the greatest positive changes in economic policy. The World Bank regards this as one of the main indicators of the positive effects of policy adjustments desired by the Bank. The World Bank does note – in agreement with the IMF – that investment and savings do not respond to the adjustment programmes. The message of the entire study, however, is that the adjustments did have great positive effects.

Rather a lot can be said against this conclusion, though. For example, the scoring system on the basis of which the division into groups is made refers to only a few elements of the adjustment programmes. The total score on fiscal policy has been based merely on the improvement of the government budget deficit and the change in tax revenues; the score on monetary policy has been based largely on the change in inflation; and the score on exchange rate policy has been based to an important extent on the changes in the real exchange rate. The measures relating to trade policy, like the decrease in regulations concerning the distribution of foreign currency, eliminating non-tariff-related restrictions, and reforming tariffs, have not been included in the analysis. Moreover, important measures relating to agricultural policy, like restructuring marketing boards, have been left out of consideration. Thus, the analysis cannot possibly judge the suitability of the adjustments recommended by the World Bank. A significant criticism is furthermore the fact that countries are granted points on the basis of the development of variables that cannot be controlled directly by the government, that is endogenous variables. Thus, a decrease of inflation is considered an improvement in economic policy. However, a decrease in inflation could be rather the result of a particular government policy. It could very well be that this decrease in inflation has been caused by an economic measure that does not correspond with World Bank wishes, like the introduction of price control. The same criticism refers to the other variables the scoring system has been based on. Moreover, the same items may be granted points twice. Countries are granted points on the basis of how inflation and the real exchange rate evolve. However, these variables affect each other directly. After all, the real exchange rate equals the nominal exchange rate after correcting for price differences at home and abroad. Especially with respect to the countries in the CFA zone, which did not experience any adjustment of the nominal exchange rate during this period, double granting of points is conceivable.

Also when the method of scoring points is accepted, the World Bank conclusion that a 'good' policy results in good economic achievements impels the necessary differentiations. What is rather striking, for example, is the fact that there seems to be no relation between an improvement in agricultural growth and an improvement in the economic policy, according to this World Bank scoring system. This is particularly worrying since stimulation of the agricultural sector is one of the main objectives of World Bank adjustment programmes. The World Bank explains this result by pointing out the fact that it does take some time before policy reforms lead to higher prices for producers in the agricultural sector. Moreover, the short-term supply elasticity of agricultural production with respect to price rises is small. In the long term these elasticities are said to be much larger. According to the Bank, the short-term analysis thus underestimates the long-term positive effects.

In order to be able to analyse better the relation between economic policy and a growth in agricultural production, the World Bank also developed a standard for the real protection of the agricultural sector. This standard is determined by means of a comparison of the price farmers receive for their agricultural exports and the world market price expressed in the domestic currency, taking into account the ratio between the actual nominal and equilibrium exchange rate. An increase in the real protection coefficient is associated with a decrease in the degree to which the government taxes the agricultural sector, that is a more positive policy as regards the agricultural sector. The World Bank notes a positive relation between agricultural growth and an increase in the protection coefficient and considers this to be an indicator of the supposition that a 'good' policy leads to fine economic achievements. Again, a lot can be said against this conclusion. For instance, establishing a protection coefficient is rather precarious, as the World Bank itself observes too. In particular since the equilibrium exchange rate is not observable and therefore must be estimated. Moreover, the increase in agricultural growth turns out to be largest in the Ivory Coast and in Chad. In both countries the protection coefficient decreased severely, which, according to the World Bank, is exactly an indicator of a deterioration of policy concerning the agricultural sector.

A number of outcomes of the World Bank study does indeed strongly contradict the positive relation between a 'good' policy and favourable economic achievements as stressed by the Bank. For example, first, Mozambique, which according to the World Bank is among the countries with a deterioration of economic policy, realised the largest increase in the growth of per capita GDP and the investment/GDP ratio; second, Madagascar and Gabon – ranked among the countries with a slight improvement in economic policy and a deterioration in economic policy respectively – realised the greatest increase in growth of exports; third, Tanzania – which, according to the World Bank scoring system, after Ghana realised the greatest positive change in economic policy – is actually among the countries with the largest deterioration of the savings/GDP ratio.

Finally, one must also take into account the fact that the apparent improvement in the economic situation of Africa is quite small, with the exception of a few countries. For example, the average industrial growth of the group of countries with the greatest improvement in economic policy merely increased from 1.8 per cent to 1.9 per cent. Moreover, the average growth of per capita GDP in these countries is still very low: 1.1 per cent. The average growth of per capita GDP in the countries with a slight improvement in the economic policy is even negative: −0.1 per cent.

Studies based on the 'with or without' method

A second method is the 'with or without' approach. In this method the course of several relevant variables for countries that have implemented an adjustment programme is compared with the course of the same variables in countries without adjustment programmes. The problems involved in the 'before and after' method also apply to this approach. An additional, implicit assumption of the 'with or without' method is that the different countries are comparable, irrespective of the adjustment programmes. Often it appears that only poorly achieving countries contract a reform programme while countries with better achievements will be able to cope without any help. Elbadawi (1992, p. 44), for example, argues that countries that implemented a World Bank reform programme had relatively weaker economies in the early 1980s. Moreover, the different groups of countries may be faced with totally different exogenous influences during the period of adjustment. Differences in outcome may thus be caused by intrinsic differences between two groups. There are certain ways to restrict these problems, though. For example, the differences between the groups can be determined prior to introducing a programme so that they may be taken into account during further analyses. In addition to the differences between the groups, countries that implement a reform programme are often not a homogenous set. The degree of implementation of reform programmes and the economic achievements strongly differ, which lead to increasing unreliability of data. Again it is not clear what influence is actually measured. A possible solution to this problem may be the further segmentation of the groups. Naturally, this must be done prior to and regardless of the empirical outcomes.

The World Bank evaluated the adjustment programmes in a series of earlier reports (World Bank, 1988, 1990b, 1992a). In these reports the Bank's adjustment programmes on the various continents are analysed, using a combination of the 'before and after' and the 'with or without' method. Since the analysis and the outcomes of the analysis show many similarities to Elbadawi (1992) and Elbadawi *et al.* (1992) I shall restrict the discussion to these latter studies.

In two comparable studies (Elbadawi, 1992; Elbadawi *et al.*, 1992) the World Bank adjustment programmes are evaluated. These authors distinguish three sets of countries: early intensive-adjustment lending countries, that is countries that have had two or more SALs or three or more adjustment loans (SALs and SECALs) in 1985 or earlier; other adjustment-lending countries; and non-adjustment-lending countries. Contrary to the World Bank (1994a), the division is based on the number of loans that were contracted rather than on the degree to which policy adjustments have been executed.

The outcomes of Elbadawi's study for the African countries are presented in Table 7.3, which shows that the growth of GDP for the intensive-adjustment-lending countries increased sharply during the second half of the 1980s, whereas the growth of GDP in countries that did not adjust decreased. In all three groups investment decreased in relation to GDP. What is rather striking is that this decrease was largest in the group of intensive-adjustment-lending countries. Savings in relation to GDP decreased stronger in the intensive-adjustment-lending countries than in other adjustment-lending countries. In those countries where adjustments were not implemented the rate of savings improved. In agreement with Schadler *et al.* (1993) and the World Bank (1994a), this study, too, points out the disappointing results concerning investment and savings. Exports in relation to GDP increased during the 1980s in the intensive-adjustment-lending countries, whereas this share decreased in the two other sets of countries. Elbadawi (1992) also studies the development of inflation. It appears that the non-adjustment-lending countries perform best; here inflation decreased by an average 5 per cent during the 1985–89 period. Also for the intensive-adjustment-lending countries inflation decreased but is still very high at an average 15 per cent in the 1985–89 period.

Mosley and Weeks (1993) also distinguish groups of intensive-adjustment-lending countries, other adjustment-lending countries, and non-adjustment-lending countries. However, in addition, they present results with respect to countries that have adjusted to some extent. For example, in the group of intensive-adjustment-lending countries they abstract from Nigeria, and in the group of other adjustment-lending countries four war-stricken countries are excluded (Ethiopia, Liberia, Somalia and Sudan). Like Elbadawi's analysis (1992), this analysis also shows that the intensive-adjustment-lending countries realised a strong growth of GDP. However, it also appears that the results of the intensive-adjustment-lending countries – excluding Nigeria – are no better than those of the other adjustment-lending countries. This is even more true after correcting for the specific influence of the war-stricken countries in the group of the other adjusting countries.

Mosley and Weeks (1993), subsequently, make a new division of countries based on the emphasis of certain elements in the programmes. The study suggests that the World Bank programmes had a favourable effect on exports, since, with respect to

Table 7.3 A comparison of different groups of adjusting countries in Africa

	1970–80 growth GDP	1981–84 growth GDP	1985–89 growth GDP	1970–80 Inv/GDP	1981–1984 Inv/GDP	1985–89 Inv/GDP
EAL	3.7	0.1	3.7	24.7	18.4	16.9
OAL	3.2	3.1	3.0	20.5	21.5	18.7
NAL	6.0	4.5	2.3	21.1	18.2	17.3
	Sav/GDP	Sav/GDP	Sav/GDP	Exp/GDP	Exp/GDP	Exp/GDP
EAL	16.1	9.9	11.0	30.2	27.7	29.6
OAL	6.4	5.9	5.3	21.0	19.6	18.5
NAL	12.8	10.6	15.0	30.2	32.9	30.3

Source: Elbadawi, 1992, Table 2.4

Notes: EAL: early intensive-adjustment lending countries; OAL: other adjustment-lending countries; NAL: non-adjustment-lending countries.

all subgroups of adjusting countries, this growth of exports exceeds the growth of exports in the group of countries that did not participate in any adjustment programme. The results with regard to investment and growth of GDP are disappointing, though: for three out of five subgroups of countries with adjustment programmes, growth of investment and growth of GDP is lower than for the group of countries without adjustment programmes.

Mosley and Weeks (1993) further investigate the factors that determine the success of the reforms by subdividing the groups on the basis of the measures taken and the main points of the reform programmes. They conclude that economic recovery is primarily dependent on a consistent developmental policy. From their point of view, a consistent developmental policy consists of trade liberalisation with a devaluation of the currency, or liberalisation of the agricultural sector with an increase in government investment. Mosley and Weeks (1993) state that, first, trade liberalisation without devaluation of the currency will result in poor achievements. Since, in this case, trade liberalisation would lead to a direct increase in imports while exports are not promoted; second, liberalisation of the agricultural sector will only have positive effects if it goes together with an increase in government expenditure for capital goods. If the infrastructure and marketing facilities are not maintained, the stimulating effect of market incentives will not lead to an increase in production; third, the economic achievements of countries without World Bank adjustment programmes where the currency was devalued and government investment had increased are better than the economic achievements of countries with World Bank adjustment programmes where the currency was not devaluated and government investment did not increase.

A study by some researchers of the IMF (Hadjimichael *et al.*, 1995) compares economic performance of different subgroups of countries in Africa. This study distinguishes between countries with low macroeconomic imbalances, sustained adjusters and countries with protracted macroeconomic imbalances. The countries in the first group did not need an adjustment programme of the IMF or the World Bank since they already implemented appropriate policies. A country is classified in the second group when a positive change in the economic policy has taken place under an IMF adjustment programme. Countries in the third group did not adopt appropriate policy changes. The study shows, for the 1986–93 period, that the sustained adjusters and the countries with low macro economic imbalances performed better in terms of GDP growth rates, export growth rates, import growth rates and investment ratios than the countries with protracted imbalances. Therefore, the study concludes that 'good' policies in line with the IMF and World Bank adjustment programmes pay off in terms of better economic performance.[3] However, in my view, this conclusion needs more in-depth research. For instance, the results refer to the average outcome per group so that it does not become clear whether this conclusion holds for most individual countries. Moreover, it appears that the countries with protracted imbalances performed better with respect to savings and inflation than the sustained adjustment countries. Finally, the exact criteria for the country groupings are unclear. With respect to the latter, it is interesting to compare the country grouping of the IMF (Hadjimichael *et al.*, 1995) with that of the World Bank (1994a). The most striking differences are the following. First, two of the six countries (Burkina Faso and Nigeria) classified by the World Bank as countries with large positive improvements in the economic policy are classified by the IMF as countries with protracted imbalances. Second, three of the twelve countries (Benin, Mozambique and Togo) classified by the World Bank as countries with a deterioration of the economic policy, are classified by the IMF as sustained adjusters with appropriate policies.

Studies based on the regression method

A third method, the so-called 'regression method', tries to measure the effect of adjustment programmes by using the (elements of the) programmes as an explanatory independent variable in a cross-section regression comparison. The method has several great advantages. Applying it, one can determine the extent of the influence of a policy variable; a quantitive analysis is made possible. The influence of other – non-programme-related – variables can now also be determined. Finally, the significance of the measures taken can be determined, that is apart from the funds offered, that is the adjustment loan. A drawback of this approach, however, is the fact that a useful regression analysis is hardly practicable since often African data are rather inadequate.

Elbadawi (1992) and Elbadawi *et al.* (1992) use the regression method to determine the contribution of reform programmes to the economy. They use an advanced method to determine the equations to be eventually estimated. I shall not explain their method elaborately but some remarks will be made, though. One of the characteristics of Elbadawi's method is that the decision to participate in adjustment programmes is made endogenous. The effect of the adjustment programmes is determined in two steps. First, an equation is estimated where the decision whether or not to join an adjustment programme is the dependent variable. The outcomes of this estimation are subsequently used in the regressions with which the effects of the programmes on the various macroeconomic variables are determined. Table 7.4 presents the outcomes of the estimations for Africa. I shall present only the coefficient which refers to the adjustment programmes. It appears that the adjustment programmes have a statistically significant, positive effect on exports, and a statistically significant, negative one on investment. No other significant influence on any of the entities studied could be discerned.

Table 7.4 Results of adjustment programmes: regression method

change in growth GDP	−0.014 (−0.830)
change in exports/GDP ratio	0.080 (2.459)
change in investment/GDP ratio	−0.084 (−2.314)
change in savings/GDP ratio	−0.083 (−1.574)
change in inflation	0.122 (1.244)

Source: Elbadawi, 1992, Table 4.3

Note: Numbers in parentheses are t-values.

Mosley *et al.* (1991) also investigate the effectiveness of the programmes by means of the regression analysis. Characteristic of their analysis is that they distinguish between the degree to which the programmes have been implemented and the loans related to the programmes. Thus the effect of the adjustment programmes can be separated from the effect of the loans.

It turns out that the financial means supplied by the World Bank and the IMF have had only a significant effect on the growth of exports and the growth of imports. It is rather striking that the World Bank adjustment loans initially even had a negative effect on the growth of exports. The cause of this could be that several countries could actually postpone the necessary adjustments exactly because the World Bank granted them financial means. The degree of implementation of World Bank policy requirements appears to have a positive effect on the growth of GDP after one year and on the growth of imports and exports initially. After a year, however, the World Bank policy requirements affect negatively the growth of imports and exports. According to the estimations, the adjustment programmes have no effect at all on investment and foreign private capital flows. According to Mosley *et al.* (1991), the principal conclusion to be drawn from their study is that World Bank loans have an adverse effect on the goal variables whereas the extent to which policy requirements have been implemented has had a positive effect. The empirical results are not very satisfactory from a statistical point of view. Only some variables prove to have a significant influence; the explanatory powers of the equation is small in many cases; and some outcomes are difficult to interpret. For example, it is hard to explain why the implementation of the policy conditions has a negative influence on exports after one year. Mosley *et al.* (1991) think that this could be the result of the negative effect of the policy programmes on investment, which after some time have an adverse effect on exports. For Africa this cannot be the case though, since their study shows that the implementation of the policy conditions does not have a significant effect on investment.

7.3 Conclusions

Table 7.5 compares the outcomes of the different studies, as far as this is possible. I shall consider only the effects of the adjustment programmes on GDP, exports, investment and savings since these are the only variables practically all studies have included. The table shows that, with respect to the variables I distinguished, a unanimous answer cannot be given to the question whether the adjustment programmes have had a positive or a negative effect. Most studies suggest that the adjustment programmes had a positive effect on the growth of GDP. On the basis of the above, one could – with some reserves – state that some improvement in economic growth may be observed after reforms. The results with regard to exports are extremely divided. The studies conducted by the IMF and Elbadawi's 'with or without' method imply that there is an adverse effect of the adjustment programmes on exports, whereas the World Bank, Mosley and Weeks, and Elbadawi's regression analysis suggest a positive relation. Also with respect to investment and savings, the effec ment programmes are not clear. Some studies suggest that there may b relation, whereas other studies observe a negative relation or no rela Besides, with respect to both variables one must take into consideration th fact that if there is a positive effect at all, this effect will be quite limited. Even the IMF and the World Bank note that the effects of reforms on savings and investment are disappointing. This could be a dubious development with respect to future economic growth.

The methodological problems related to the various studies are actually so very large that no concrete conclusions can be drawn. Especially the 'before and after' and the 'with or without' method, which are used by the World Bank and the IMF, can tell us only what happened rather than why it happened. The 'regression analysis' enables one to quantify better the relations between the adjustment programmes and macroeconomic variables. It is, therefore, rather discouraging that the most advanced study based on this method – that is, Elbadawi's – does not observe a significant effect of

Table 7.5 Results of adjustment programmes: an overview

	GDP	Exp.	Inv.	Sav.
Before and after method				
IMF1	+	–	+	+
IMFT	+	–	+/–	+
World Bank1	+	+	+	+
World BankT	+/–	+	+/–	+/–
With or without method				
Elbadawi	+	–	–	–
Mosley and Weeks	+	+	+	n.a.
IMF	+	+	+	–
Regression method				
Elbadawi	0	+	–	0
Mosley, Harrigan and Toye	+	+/–	0	n.a.

Notes: Before and after method: + (–) if percentage of countries with an improvement of > 55% (< 45%). +/– 45% < percentage < 55%. IMF1 (IMFT) refers to group 1 (total) in Schadler *et al.*, 1993. World Bank1 (World BankT) refers to group 1 (total). With or without method: + (–) if adjusting countries perform better (worse) than nonadjusting countries. Elbadawi: comparison refers to EAL versus NAL during 1985–89. Mosley and Weeks: result refers to comparison of countries with comprehensive programmes and countries without adjustment programmes. IMF: comparison refers to sustained adjusters and low macroeconomic imbalances countries versus countries with protracted imbalances for the 1986–1993 period (Hadjimichael *et al.*, 1995). Regression method: + (–) significantly positive (negative) effect; 0 no significant effect; +/– initially positive, later negative. Mosley, Harrigan and Toye: result refers to the relation between the degree of implementation of the programmes and the macroeconomic variables distinguished.

the programmes on the growth of GDP and savings, but rather a significantly negative effect of the programmes on investment.

The extremely positive note concerning the effectiveness of adjustment programmes, expressed by the World Bank (1994a), seems to have been based on its faith in the positive effect of the policy adjustments it considers desirable rather than on concrete empirical outcomes. In my view, a judgement on the suitability of structural adjustment programmes requires more in-depth research into the functioning of the policy adjustments considered advisable by the Bank and the IMF. In this respect, what I find rather promising would be a method of research that has not been applied often but has become slightly more common recently. Several scientists and a number of international institutions are working on simulation models to determine the effectiveness of adjustment programmes.[4] This simulation method is not that simple since a model must be developed first. The approach, however, has a large number of advantages since most of the above-mentioned problems involved in the other methods no longer arise. One no longer has to consider only those countries with adjustment programmes in order to determine the effectiveness of an adjustment programme in a particular country. Moreover, the problem that some countries do not implement a complete programme does not affect the analysis any longer. Also this method can distinguish the influence of various programmes and the effects of a financial contribution. World Bank and IMF adjustment programmes can be analysed for individual countries. Simulations can be used to determine the perfect set of policy adjustments for each country. The package of measures suggested by the World Bank and the IMF may after all be successful in one country and a total failure in another. This brings us back to the remark I made in Chapter 3: the desirability of a certain policy may depend on the stage of development of a particular country. Finally, with the simulation method one can consider the relation between policy instruments and policy objectives. In this context the method will provide more information on how programmes function in contrast to certain approaches that will consider results only.

Notes

1 This chapter is based on Lensink and Vijselaar (1995).
2 Bouton *et al.* (1994) update the results of World Bank (1994a). Since the methodology and the results of this study are the same as in World Bank (1994a) I restrict the analysis to the latter study.
3 This conclusion is also based on an econometric investigation.
4 Mosley *et al.* (1991, Ch. 8) present outcomes of simulations for Malawi and Morocco. Recently, the World Bank too developed several models that can be used to analyse adjustment programmes for individual countries (see Section 5.3).

8 Adjustment programmes, social relations and the environment

In the previous chapter attention was paid to the extent to which the adjustment programmes stimulate economic progress. The World Bank and the IMF are pleased with the economic results of the programmes, whereas critics stress the fact that the economic results of the programmes are disappointing. The most severe criticism of structural adjustment programmes, however, does not centre on the possibly slight economic results but rather on the social consequences of the programmes. This chapter will also concentrate on this issue. Furthermore, an alternative adjustment programme will be presented in accordance with the critics' demands.

The World Bank and the IMF, in particular during the early stages of adjustment, argued that a capitalist economy with full competition is the best way to guarantee an improvement in prosperity. Theoretic evidence for this line of reasoning is presented by means of Pareto's welfare theory. In Section 8.1 a brief outline of this theory is presented since the discussion with respect to the effects of adjustment programmes on the environment and income distribution frequently apply insights based on Pareto's welfare economics. Subsequently, the critics' points of view will be discussed. The adjustment programmes do not lead to sustained development, according to the critics of the World Bank and the IMF. The adjustment programmes aim primarily at solving short-term problems while the long-term issues are practically neglected. According to the critics, the environment is severely damaged, income distribution becomes increasingly unequal, and the issue of poverty becomes more pressing due to the programmes (Sections 8.2 and 8.3). They also argue that the adjustment programmes cause the position of women to be marginalised (Section 8.4). The alternative adjustment programmes pay quite some attention to the above factors (Section 8.5). Section 8.6 contains a summary of this chapter.

8.1 Welfare economics

In this book, I have already mentioned several times that the World Bank and the IMF presuppose that a capitalist economy without price control will lead to efficient allocation of means of production and optimum welfare to society as a whole. But what exactly is an efficient allocation of means of production, and why will a capitalist economy result in the efficient allocation of means of production?

Welfare economics investigates the conditions that guarantee a maximum welfare for a country as a whole. A difficulty here is how to define an increase in welfare. Usually the so-called Pareto criterion is used for this purpose. This criterion enables one to judge when a country obtains maximum welfare.

Pareto's criterion argues that there is an increase in welfare if at least one individual can realise an improvement in satisfying his or her needs without this being at the expense of another individual's utility. The optimum situation, referred to as a Pareto-efficient allocation, is achieved when no one (person) can be made better off without someone else being made worse off.

An important prerequisite of a Pareto efficient allocation is that there must be technical efficiency. This means that it is impossible to produce more of a product by means of reallocation without decreasing the production of another product. This is in fact a situation where producers produce on the production possibilities curve (see Ch. 3). When a country does not produce on the production possibilities curve, that is when there is unemployment or insufficient use of machines, an improvement of production may be realised without this affecting the production of another good. This also suggests a Pareto-inefficient allocation, since the production of the good can lead to an improvement of someone's utility without harming another individual's utility.

A situation of technical efficiency does, however, not guarantee a Pareto efficient allocation. After all, enterprises may produce goods that are not in demand. A Pareto efficient allocation therefore requires that consumer demand corresponds with the production realised by producers.

In principle, a Pareto efficient allocation can be realised by a complex process of government intervention. However, it is far more easy to let markets work. By means of Pareto's so-called optimum theorem it can be shown that in a market economy, with full competition, the price mechanism automatically causes a Pareto efficient allocation. The price mechanism brings about optimum harmony between consumer needs and the production possibilities of enterprises, optimum distribution of final products among consumers, and optimum distribution of the production among enterprises. Formal evidence for this can be found in textbooks on microeconomy (e.g. Nicholson, 1992).

Neoliberal economists, and in line with them, the World Bank and the IMF, to an important extent base their case of liberalising markets on Pareto's optimum theorem. Critics of the World Bank and the IMF, however, argue that the assumptions which form the basis of Pareto's optimum theorem do not take root in developing countries, as will be discussed in further detail later on in this chapter.

8.2 Adjustment programmes and the environment

Since the mid-1980s relatively more attention has been paid to the environmental consequences of economic development in general and of World Bank and IMF programmes in particular. Environmentalists severely criticise World Bank and IMF policy. With respect to the World Bank, criticism is primarily directed towards its project-focused policy. The environmental movement claims that the World Bank's preference for large-scale projects is disastrous to the environment. It is stated that huge dams and hydro-electric power stations are preferred over energy-saving projects. The environmentalists also stress that the evaluation of World Bank projects concerning environmental consequences is completely inadequate. Until recently, there was no possibility at all to test environmental consequences. It is rather telling that an internal World Bank report – the Wapenhans report (World Bank, 1992c) – confirms criticism by environmentalists of World Bank project policy to a significant extent (see Berg and Sherk, 1994, p. 309).[1]

Critics of the World Bank and the IMF also claim that the structural adjustment programmes would disastrously affect the environment. Following the Brundtland report (WCED, 1987), authors like George (1988, 1992) and several non-government organisations like the Environmental Defence Fund, Friends of the Earth and Probe International, stress that production growth through market reforms as desired by the World Bank and the IMF involve huge environmental costs. The World Bank and the IMF, however, argue that a negative relation between economic growth and the environment is not a matter of course. From their point of view economic growth is actually required to finance a clean production process.

George (1992) detects a direct relation between the high foreign debts of developing countries and deforestation. More generally, she states that the export-oriented developmental model by the World Bank and the IMF is responsible for damage done to the environment. High foreign debts, together with the condition related to most adjustment programmes that the indebted countries must meet their debt service, lead to developing countries being forced to increase their production of exports in the short term so that foreign currencies can be earned. Since many developing countries produce relatively cheap products that require the production factor of nature, trade liberalisation stimulates overexploitation of the production factor nature which consequently causes impoverishment of soil, desertification, and erosion of agricultural land (Opschoor, 1994). According to George (1992), the export-oriented World Bank and IMF strategy promotes large-scale agriculture which has a direct negative effect on the environment. Moreover, trade liberalisation may attract highly polluting industries to developing countries. According to critics, the export-oriented strategy furthermore stimulates an expansion of the area of land used for agriculture at the expense of rain forests. Peasants, who can no longer use the rich lands, since these are now used for the production of exports, are forced to move further into the rain forests in order to obtain a piece of farm land. George (1992) explicitly states that these 'shifting cultivators' are not responsible for large-scale deforestation. The strategy pursued by the World Bank and the IMF is the real cause. Table 8.1 presents the degree of deforestation in six African countries. Annual deforestation appears to be between 0.5 and 1.3 per cent.

The World Bank and the IMF defend their programmes by saying that an increase in trade will have a positive effect on the environment. Trade stimulates competition so that production factors are allocated more efficiently and economies of scale can be

Table 8.1 Natural forest area

	Total Area (thousand sq. km)	Total Area (thousand sq. km)	Annual deforestation 1981–90 (% of total area)
	1980	1990	
Ghana	109	96	1.3
Ivory Coast	121	109	1.0
Kenya	13	12	0.5
Madagascar	171	158	0.8
Nigeria	168	156	0.7
Tanzania	379	336	1.2

Source: World Bank, 1994b, Table 33

benefited from. In their opinion, waste is thus decreased which has a positive effect on the environment. Through the advantages of specialisation, international trade extends consumption possibilities of countries without increasing the amount of production factors required for production. The positive effect of efficiency on the environment, however, is lost due to the negative environmental effects of an increase in production, critics say.

The World Bank and the IMF argue – in agreement with the neoliberal line of reasoning and the Pareto optimum theorem – that the environment benefits from improved market forces. They feel that the waste of resources is mainly the result of lacking or inefficient markets (Opschoor, 1994, p. 95). According to the Bank and the IMF, in a properly functioning market economy the price mechanism automatically leads to an improved allocation of means of production and consequently reduce resource waste.

The environmental movement acknowledges that prices should reflect properly the costs. However, they stress that World Bank and IMF policy – aimed at 'getting prices right' by means of privatisation – did not really lead to the right prices (see Berg and Sherk, 1994; Reed, 1992). After all, when prices are determined, an enterprise does not take into account the negative environmental effects on the rest of the economy; this is called an external effect or an externality. When external effects occur, Pareto's optimum theorem does not hold true. In that case the price mechanism does not automatically lead to a Pareto efficient allocation.

An externality occurs if production or consumption by an individual affects the benefit of others. Externalities operate outside the market so that the causer of the externality does not take them into account when making decisions (Hartog, 1981, p. 142). External effects may be either positive or negative. An example of a positive external effect is the number of telephone connections. When more telephones have been connected, the benefit of having a connection increases (Hartog, 1981,

p. 143). A negative externality is when the production or consumption of a certain enterprise or individual has a negative effect on others.

If individuals do not bear the full costs or do not acquire the revenues related to their activities, this will generally result in a social sub-optimum result, a Pareto inefficient allocation. A social optimum result would take place if individual decisions were based on a weighing of all costs or revenues that relate to the activity concerned. This will be illustrated by way of an example. An entrepreneur whose production of a product involves polluting rivers (a negative externality) will ask a lower price for the product when the costs of river pollution are not eventually paid by the enterprise. In this case the price of the product will not represent all social costs. The result will be that the demand for this product and thus the production of the product exceeds the optimum volume. In an ideal situation prices also take into account the environmental costs of production and consumption. In other words, the environmental costs of projects ought to be included in price-making, that is they must be internalised. Internalising external effects in prices may be realised by means of government measures like taxes and subsidies. In the above example the government could, for example, charge the polluting enterprise pollution taxes. Thus the cost price will correspond the real total social costs. Environmentalists, however, argue that adjustment policies aimed at reducing the role of the government hamper the realisation of this objective.

Opschoor (1994), who explicitly states that the direction of the whole of environmental effects of World Bank and IMF programmes is not clear beforehand, points out several other mechanisms through which the adjustment programmes, may damage the environment. In many adjustment programmes subsidies have been abolished, and taxes and excise duties have been introduced. Consequently, relative prices are affected. The altered relative prices influence the environment directly by means of a change in the use of a product and indirectly by means of substituting other products. If, for example, subsidies for fertiliser are abolished, the price of fertiliser will go up. The use of fertiliser will fall consequently, so that fewer chemicals will be used, which is beneficial to the environment. However, at the same time the soil may be impoverished which will damage the environment. The devaluation of a currency may also have a negative effect on the environment. Devaluation often leads to a shift of production of goods for the domestic market to the production of export goods. If the cultivation of annuals increases as a result, the soil will deteriorate. If the cultivation of perennials, like coffee and tea, is stimulated, this may lead to a more sustained use of land. In other words, the direction of environmental effects depends on the type of plant to be cultivated.

As a response to the severe criticism by environmentalists, the World Bank has made several changes in its 'environmental policy' (see Brandon, 1994, p. 133; Opschoor, 1994, p. 95). During the 1970s only a few people within the World Bank studied environmental issues. Immediately after the publication of the Brundtland report a complete Environmental Department was established. Moreover, since 1993 one of the five World Bank vice-presidencies is entirely devoted to environmentally sustained development. Today, the World Bank employs approximately 200 full-time environmental specialists (Brandon, 1994, p. 133). In 1989, the World Bank developed procedures for an environmental assessment of its projects. Projects are granted an A, B or C rating. A-status refers to projects that affect the environment highly; B refers to projects that have a limited effect on the environment; and C refers to projects that do not affect the environment (Opschoor, 1994, p. 105). A-status projects require a full environmental assessment; B-status projects require only a partial assessment. The environmental assessment studies projects for their possible environmental and social effects. The number of World Bank projects aimed at improving the environment has also been extended considerably. Moreover, the World Bank supervises the global environmental facility (GEF). This facility has been introduced to provide developing countries with the financial means to reduce their environmental problems. The financial means for the GEF are deposited with the World Bank. The environmental programme by the United Nations (UNEP) and the United Nations developmental programme, however, are responsible for this facility.

George and Sabelli (1994) very much doubt whether the changes the World Bank has implemented with respect to its environmental policy actually lead to better policy. They argue that a considerable portion of World Bank staff still does not feel the need to consider the environmental aspects of their programmes. George and Sabelli argue that large-scale environment-unfriendly projects are actually carried out – despite the fact that a growing part of the World Bank is indeed concerned with environmental issues. The environmental assessment of the projects is criticised as well. Even for projects with the most strictly environmental assessment, the assessment is by no means strict enough. What is also pointed out is the fact that there is no environmental assessment at all for the structural adjustment loans (George and Sabelli, 1994, p. 165).

The World Bank states that at present economic growth in general is no longer at the centre of its programmes, but rather sustainable economic growth. The notion of sustainable refers to 'meeting the needs of the present generation without compromising the needs of the future generation' (Todaro, 1994, p. 327). In practice there is no real change whatsoever in World Bank policy, George and Sabelli (1994) feel. World Bank programmes are still primarily directed towards realising economic growth (Opschoor, 1994, p. 113). The ruling point of view is still

> growth and development first, which will bring richess, which will then allow a country to take care of the environment. . . . Promoting development is the best way to protect the environment (George and Sabelli, 1994, p. 170).

The GEF of the World Bank is also severely criticised. The policy of the facility is entirely dictated by industrialised countries. Critics state that the needs of and knowledge in developing countries are not at all taken into account.

It is difficult to objectively determine the influence of IMF and World Bank adjustment programmes on the environment. I have mentioned Opschoor's study (1994), which explains that it is theoretically impossible to predict the direction of the environmental effects of adjustment programmes. Empirical studies would have to show the effect of the programmes on the environment. However, there is a serious lack of reliable empirical studies in this field, particularly for African countries. A study by Reed (1992) provides some empirical information. He presents case studies for the Ivory Coast, Mexico and Thailand, concentrating on the effects of structural adjustment programmes on the environment. Reed's overall conclusion is that the environmental effects of the adjustment programmes are not clear. Reed, however, also concludes explicitly that the effects were in none of the countries optimal. The adjustment programmes by no means resulted in sustainable development, so that changes in the programmes in order to improve the environmental effects are desirable. He denies the correlation between high foreign debt and deforestation – as observed by George (1992) – though. According to Reed, this correlation is not as straightforward as George claims it to be. Reed also pays some attention to the so-called environmental Kuznets Curve. A frequently heard argument is that environmental pollution is an inevitable by-product of economic growth in the early stages of economic development. If a country is not that rich, it cannot afford an environment-friendly production process. With the lapse of time, when incomes increase, more money can be spent on improving the environment. According to the critics, structural adjustment programmes lead to a decrease in economic growth in the short term. Consequently, the period during which countries experience an environment-unfriendly development is protracted by means of adjustment programmes. Reed does not feel that a negative correlation between economic growth and environmental pollution is inevitable during the initial stages of economic development. The case study for the Ivory Coast, for example, shows that the realised economic growth need not have caused damage to the environment if only a better policy had been pursued.

8.3 Adjustment programmes, poverty and income distribution

Before discussing the effects of adjustment programmes on poverty and income distribution, I shall again refer to Pareto's optimum criterion. World Bank and IMF critics claim that the Pareto efficient allocation – which can be achieved in a capitalist economy with a perfectly functioning price mechanism – does not imply that income is distributed equally among subjects. For a Pareto efficient allocation can be realised after a given distribution of final goods and means of production among subjects. A different initial situation will lead to a different Pareto efficient allocation. Supposing the economy consists of two subjects, A and B; and supposing that in the initial situation subject A owns all final goods. This may signify a Pareto efficient allocation since it is impossible to improve B's utility by means of redistributing the means of production without negatively affecting A's utility. Another Pareto efficient allocation is realised if in the initial situation the goods are distributed equally among the two subjects. Despite the fact that the second situation seems preferable, Pareto's criterion cannot be applied here to make a proper evaluation. Pareto's criterion per definition cannot classify the various Pareto-efficient allocations. In other words, a capitalist market economy can be Pareto efficient and at the same time imply that a small part of the population is extremely rich whereas the majority lives below the poverty threshold. Thus an improvement in the welfare of the most poor ones that slightly compromises the welfare of the rich is not Pareto-efficient. Critics, therefore, dispute that a market economy automatically affects favourably income distribution. They feel that the government should play an important role in attempting to realise improved income distribution.

After this short digression, the effects of the adjustment programmes on poverty and income distribution will be discussed more explicitly. According to George (1992), the export-oriented World Bank and IMF policies lead to an increase in income inequality. George claims that the export-oriented strategy is profitable to a small group of landowners while the masses become increasingly poorer. The rich large landowners will use a larger part of their best land for growing export crops and they will more and more buy out peasants. In this context a direct relation with the environmental effects of adjustment programmes is frequently noted. After all, increasing poverty promotes ecological deterioration when it leads to over-exploitation of resources (Durning, 1989).

Critics claim that if an adjustment programme has any positive effect on growth at all, the poor by no means benefit from this growth. The adjustment programmes hardly contain any measures to protect the poor against the negative consequences of economic growth. Especially UNICEF (the United Nations Children's Fund) stresses that the adjustment programmes do not have a 'human face'. In the influential study *Adjustment with a Human Face* (Cornia *et al.*, 1987) it is argued that completely ignoring the social consequences of the adjustment programmes and undue emphasis on macroeconomic measures will result in the process of adjustment not matching the long-term objectives of development. In this study it is noted that the desired decrease in government expenditure has largely been realised by decreasing expenditure for education and health care. These measures specifically have negative consequences for the poor. Besides, the negative effects for the poor are intensified by charging them for government services, so that the poor have less access to education and health care.

The unfavourable effects of adjustment programmes on education and health care seem to be confirmed in Table 8.2. With respect to Africa this table shows that the number of people between the ages of 6 and 23 who received education decreased during the 1980s. Moreover, the number of people per doctor and per nurse increased strongly.[2]

The World Bank and the IMF, however, argue that the position of the poor would have deteriorated even further if adjustment programmes had not been implemented. Moreover, they are of the opinion that many adjustment programmes have been implemented only partially so that a deterioration in the situation is not the result of the adjustment programmes in themselves but rather of the implementation of the programmes. Due to the structural adjustment programmes emphasis on the urban areas decreases. Since incomes in rural areas are lower than in urban areas, and since the majority of the poor lives in the country (see Table 8.3), extra attention to these rural areas could stimulate income distribution in becoming more equitable.[3]

Husain (1994), a staff member of the World Bank, argues that adjustment programmes that pay attention to an improvement of the internal terms of trade of the agricultural sector and overall growth in agriculture offer the best opportunities for

Table 8.2 Trends in several social indicators

	Enrolment ratios	Enrolment ratios	Persons per doctor	Persons per doctor	Persons per nurse	Persons per nurse
	1980	1990	1984	1990	1984	1990
Africa	39	35	24600	35680	2200	8190
East Asia	51	54	2400	750	1500	1450
South Asia	36	45	3500	3320	2700	2960
Latin America	59	62	1200	1210	1000	1880
Ghana	48	46	14900	25000	600	2750
Ivory Coast	39	37	—	16670	—	3470
Kenya	62	58	10100	71430	1000	22320
Madagascar	60	40	10000	8330	—	2380
Nigeria	50	37	8000	66670	1000	11110
Tanzania	44	32	—	33330	—	4570

Sources: UN, 1994, Tables 4, 12 and 51; UN, 1990, Tables 11 and 23

Notes: Enrolment ratios measure the number of students enrolled in a level of education as a percentage of the population of the ages 6–23. With respect to the number of people per doctor and per nurse the figure for 1984 for East Asia refers to East Asia and Southeast Asia.

Table 8.3 Number of people living in absolute poverty (millions, 1992)

Country	Total	Rural
Ghana	6.7	5.6
Kenya	13.2	10.4
Madagascar	5.5	4.8
Nigeria	46.4	37.2
Tanzania	16.2	13.1

Source: UN, 1994, Table 3

dealing with the issue of poverty. According to Husain, the significance of the agricultural sector was insufficiently acknowledged in the early 1980s – while Husain feels that there are actually sufficient opportunities to expand production through intensification, even if environmental restrictions are taken into account when exploiting farm land. By means of devaluations, liberalisation of marketing organisations, higher producer prices, and reduced taxes, the adjustment programmes attempt to end the unfavourable situation within the agricultural sector. This will have a positive effect on income distribution, according to Husain. Critics, however, feel that this line of reasoning completely neglects income distribution within sectors. It is rather conceivable that income distribution in rural areas will become more unequal and that urban poverty increases due to structural adjustment. To the poor, higher agricultural prices do not necessarily signify an improvement of their situation.

Moreover, there seems to be a contrast between World Bank project policy and its structural adjustment policy. Despite the great store the World Bank claims to set by an improvement in growth in the agricultural sector, with respect to its project policy, loans for the benefit of agriculture and rural development have decreased strongly. Tims (1994) presents a survey of World Bank policy concerning poverty. Until the early 1970s it was assumed that the fruits of economic growth would trickle down naturally on the poor. An autonomous policy on the poverty issue was not considered to be necessary. In 1973, policy changed drastically under influence of the then World Bank president McNamara. Economic growth was said not to reach the poor automatically, and therefore a poverty policy was to be developed. Initially, this policy aimed at peasants primarily. The share of the total of loans to agriculture and rural areas increased strongly between 1968 and 1981. After 1981, attention concerning poverty was shifted from support for peasants to activities in the field of social infrastructure, like primary education, health care, drinking water supply and sanitation. Tims (1994, p. 160) argues that the most important change during the last decade refers to the significant decrease in the share of agriculture and rural development. In this sector in particular, Tims claims, poverty policy was to make a difference, while figures seem to suggest that this objective was abandoned in the 1980s. The policy concerned with poverty was increasingly directed towards the urban areas and less towards the country (Tims, 1994, p. 162).

Despite the development of an autonomous World Bank poverty policy the central notion was still that economic growth was the prime condition for fighting poverty. The World Bank and the IMF consider stimulating the market economy to be the best guarantee for reducing poverty in the long term. They do, however, acknowledge that a Pareto-efficient allocation does not automatically imply that income is distributed equally. They feel that a better income distribution can only be realised if there is actually something to distribute. A better allocation of means of production will contribute to this. Critics, however, doubt seriously whether free markets will be able to supply the basic needs of every person.

During the first adjustment period no attention was paid to social aspects, since it was assumed that adjustment programmes would not have any serious social consequences. Later, the World Bank decided to combat poverty through social programmes and other direct measures. The adjustment programmes started to concentrate more on social (temporary) provisions and restructuring government expenditure for (basic) social services. The granting of loans has been increasingly linked to progress in the fight against poverty. Furthermore, the World Bank initiated the Social Dimensions Adjustment (SDA) programme as a response to the severe criticism. The SDA programme is part of the Africa department of the World Bank but is funded by donors. The programme centres on conducting research into the effects of the adjustment programmes on poverty. Despite these policy adjustments by the World Bank, critics remain extremely sceptical. They are of the opinion that the emphasis is still too much on privatisation and economic growth and too little on basic health care and primary education.

The IMF, too, is now paying more attention to the social consequences of the adjustment programmes but is still focusing mainly on the importance of the right relative prices and institutional reforms. Moreover, the Fund does not feel that there is clear evidence of its programmes affecting income distribution. According to the IMF, income distribution is really a domestic issue and therefore does not come under its policy.

The slight attention paid to the social and human consequences of World Bank and IMF structural adjustment programmes is also the result of the process in which the programmes are drawn up, according to the critics. Only a limited number of decision-making institutions within a country are consulted, usually under pressure of time. The result of this is that the often complex and not immediately noticeable consequences are ignored. This is actually the very same criticism as formulated by those organisations that criticise the IMF and the World Bank for their poor environmental policy.

What then can be learned from the empirical and theoretical studies into the critics' claim that adjustent programmes lead to poverty and income inequality? In a number of successive articles – as part of an OECD project – Bourguignon studies the effects of the adjustment programmes on income distribution. Bourguignon, de Melo and Suwa (1991) developed a simulation model for an archetypal African country and an archetypal Latin American country. The simulations with these models suggest that a standard set of adjustments leads to an increase in income inequality in Latin America, whereas income distribution in Africa is said to improve. The positive effect in Africa is especially ascribed to the positive effects of the adjustment programmes on rural incomes, from which the poor in particular benefit. The flexibility that is thought to exist within the archetypal model for Africa stimulates the poor to increase their real agricultural income through higher revenues from exports after a real depreciation of the currency. Bourguignon *et al.* (1992) have developed a simulation model for a representative middle-income country. The strictly theoretical exercises suggest that an alternative adjustment programme – in agreement with the criticism – will not have a better effect on income distribution than World Bank and IMF programmes. In the short term the effects of the alternative programme will be better than those of the World Bank/IMF programme. In the long term, however, there is no significant difference. Bourguignon, de Melo and Morrisson (1991), on the other hand, point out the large differences with respect to the effects of the adjustment programmes. Among other things, it is concluded that especially in the Ivory Coast an alternative adjustment programme would have more favourable effects on income distribution than a standard set of adjustment measures. The overall conclusion to be drawn from the empirical studies, however, is that in this field too it is impossible to generalise the consequences of the adjustment programmes: in some countries the programmes did not affect income distribution adversely whereas in other countries income distribution has grown more unequitable due to the adjustment programmes.

8.4 Adjustment programmes and the role of women

Women play a significant role in the African economies, in particular in the agricultural sector. Most activities related to the self-sufficient agriculture, like sowing, weeding and harvesting, are done by women. In addition, women also play a significant role in the production of tradable agricultural products – cash crops. Moreover, the processing of agricultural products is mainly taken care of by women. Women pound corn and look after the cattle. Estimates show that African women, in addition to household work, are responsible for 60 to 80 per cent of labour in the agricultural sector (Todaro, 1994, p. 301). Lele (1991, pp. 49–50) states that, due to the existence of polygamy, African women play an even greater role in the rural economy than women in Asia or Latin America. Because of the extremely important role of women in Africa's agricultural production, the effects of adjustment programmes on women are of great importance.

If agricultural production aims more at the market, in accordance with World Bank and IMF wishes, this will have a great effect on the role of women. The general idea with critics is that commercialisation involves a marginalisation of the role of women in the economy. During the transformation of a traditional economy to a modern industrial economy, women are said to play an increasingly smaller role. This line of reasoning has very much been stimulated by an influential publication by Boserup (1970). According to Boserup, economic development involves an increasing degree of labour distribution in which activities that could be done at home in the traditional economy are transferred to companies. Men, who are generally better educated and who have fewer family obligations, are probably more capable of benefiting from the described development. The possibility to plan one's day does not exist in factories as much as it does at home. Women with many obligations with respect to, for example, their children are less likely to be able to take up a position in the industrial sector in comparison with men. This development is intensified since companies hire fewer women, because they are afraid of having to make additional costs with respect to pregnancies and the consequent loss of labour hours.

In Africa, especially men are in charge of production and income in commercial agriculture – cash crops – whereas women in particular take care of production and income for private ends – food crops (Lele, 1991, p. 51). Therefore, critics say, men mainly benefit from the commercialisation of agriculture. This is reinforced by the fact that only men have access to most credit facilities to stimulate commercial production. The production of cash crops at the expense of food crops will lead to the deterioration of the position of women, according to the critics. Moreover, it is argued that stimulating the production for the market by means of price rises leads to women having to work much harder. Women are more or less forced to increase the production for the market and at the same time they must maintain self-sufficient production. The additional efforts related to production for the market will be partially at the expense of the women's other activites, like raising the children and cooking. The increased prices for agricultural products also result in many women being forced to find extra jobs. Often women tried to earn the required additional income in the informal sector. Again, women would do the poorly paid activities in the informal sector. The better-paid activities in the informal sector, like repairing vehicles, were monopolised by men, partly because women had a less favourable initial position than men due to the lack of education and starting capital (Nzomo, 1992, p. 110).

The structural adjustment programmes also affect women negatively due to cuts in government expenditure. According to the critics, the decrease in expenditure for social services struck women more seriously since it was especially women who were active in this field (Cornia *et al.*, 1987; Nzomo, 1992). They argue that the adjustment programmes led to many female teachers, nurses and civil servants being fired. Moreover, it is claimed that the decrease in social expenditure led to an increasing pressure of work for women, since they very much had to compensate for the loss of social services.

Nzomo (1992, p. 112) stresses the fact that women are poorly represented in the legislative power and other powerful political decision-making organisations. Therefore, they can hardly influence the development of the adjustment programmes, let alone give the programmes a more female-dominated character.

Summarising, one may conclude that, according to the critics, the structural adjustment programmes have a negative effect on the social and economic position of women since women are among the poorest section of the population, having little private property, barely any political power, and being responsible for food production and housekeeping as well (see also Vickers, 1991).

More recently several authors have also stressed that economic development, in agreement with the World Bank and IMF idea, involves an increasing role for women in the production process. This view has been highly influenced by developments in Asia. During the 1970s, many Asian countries saw a shift from production for the domestic market to production for the foreign market. Women are more likely to participate in production for the export market since their wages are lower than men's wages. Moreover, women are said to be more capable of doing the monotonous work that is often involved in producing exports. It is also said that companies tend to employ women rather than men since women are less likely to become members of trade unions. The critics, however, stress that this development – if it catches on in Africa at all – does indeed involve extremely poor working conditions for women.

In connection with the above, supporters of the World Bank and IMF view argue that the development of export-processing zones in some structural adjustment programmes, like Kenya, are especially beneficial to women since women in particular are employed in these zones. In this context too, critics point out the poor working conditions in these sectors. Moreover, the critics argue that jobs in this sector are insecure. Any small incident may close the zones down again (Nzomo, 1992).

Despite the fact that the critics emphasise that structural adjustment programmes do not distinguish between sexes, it is acknowledged that the deterioration of living conditions of women are not merely the result of these programmes. Nzomo points out the long-standing tradition of male-dominated politics in many African countries. The adjustment programmes perpetuate these politics. She states that:

> Kenyan women, like women elsewhere, were disadvantaged even before the onset of SAPs. In other words, gender inequities and various forms of discriminatory conventions and practices against women pre-date SAPs [. . .] the significance of SAPs' impact on Kenyan (and other African) women consists in the fact that it affirms that the dominant international capitalist forces cannot be expected to alleviate the impoverished and marginalized status of women. If anything, the

> combination of the dominant male ideology and exploitative tendencies of capitalism are likely to spell doom rather than salvation for woman (Nzomo, 1992, p. 170).[4]

It is hardly possible to conduct an empirical research which presents a comparison between the effects of adjustment programmes on men and women, due to a great shortage of data. To conclude this section I present Table 8.4 in which several variables for men and women are compared. Naturally, no conclusions can be drawn with respect to the gender effects of the adjustment programmes from this table.

8.5 An alternative adjustment programme

Various organisations and individual researchers have developed alternative adjustment programmes. Examples are *The Lagos Plan of Action for the Economic Development of Africa, 1980–2000 (LPA)* (OAU, 1980), the *African Alternative Framework to Structural Adjustment Programmes for Socio-Economic Recovery and Transformation* (AAF) (ECA, 1989)[5] and 'An Alternative Approach for the Development of Africa in the 1990s and Beyond' (Cornia *et al.*, 1992). Alternative

Table 8.4 Female–male gaps

	Female share of labour force (%)	Female share of labour force (%)	Literacy	Literacy	Life expectancy at birth (years)	Life expectancy at birth (years)
	1970	1992	1970	1992	1970	1992
Africa	40	37	42	60	46 (43)	53 (50)
East Asia	41	42	—	75	60 (58)	69 (66)
South Asia	26	22	41	53	48 (50)	61 (60)
Latin America	22	27	91	95	63 (58)	71 (65)
Ghana	42	40	42	73	51 (48)	58 (54)
Ivory Coast	38	34	38	60	46 (43)	59 (53)
Kenya	42	39	43	—	52 (48)	61 (57)
Madagascar	42	39	77	83	47 (44)	53 (50)
Nigeria	37	34	40	65	43 (40)	54 (50)
Tanzania	51	47	38	—	47 (44)	52 (49)

Sources: Female share of labour force, which relates to the extent to which women are employed in the formal sector, and life expectancy at birth: World Bank (1994b, Table 29); Literacy: UN (1994, Tables 9 and 51). Literacy measures the percentage of persons aged 15 and over who can read and write. This variable is expressed in relation to the male average, which is indexed to 100. The smaller the figure, the bigger the gap. The figures in brackets refer to male life expectancy.

programmes are also discussed in *Alternative Development Strategies in Sub-Saharan Africa* (Stewart *et al.*, 1991), *Adjustment with a Human Face* (Cornia *et al.*, 1987) and 'Are Adjustment Policies in Africa Consistent with Long-Run Development Needs?' (Stewart, 1994). In this section I shall present a summary of the most important elements of these alternative programmes. I shall refer mainly to Cornia *et al.* (1992), because this UNICEF study contains many elements that are emphasised in practically all alternative programmes.

The objective of most alternative strategies is to realise sustainable and fair long-term development; a policy aimed at 'human development' is at the forefront. The alternative adjustment programmes also account for the effects on the environment, poverty and women – in agreement with the above-mentioned criticism. The World Bank and IMF policy recommendations are rejected since they do not take into account typically African conditions. The alternative programmes point out the weak production structures – there are hardly any linkages between the agricultural and the industrial sector – the existence of imperfect markets, dependence on a few different export goods only, underdeveloped institutions, the urban bias in African policies, and the partiality to the richer strata in society. The World Bank and IMF point of view that the African balance of payments deficits are especially caused by an over-expansive domestic policy, overvalued currencies and trade restrictions is contradicted. According to the alternative adjustment programmes, the deficits in the balance of payments are rather a result of external factors like deteriorating terms of trade for primary products, the increasing burden of debt, and the decrease in foreign capital inflows.

The main focus of the alternative plans will be discussed on the basis of four elements (see Cornia *et al.*, 1992):

- an agricultural strategy aimed at peasants and women
- improvement of linkages between agriculture and industry
- a policy aimed at sustainable human development
- an external policy aimed at selective protection and regional import substitution.

An agricultural strategy aimed at peasants and women

The critics acknowledge that the disregard of the agricultural sector was one of the main mistakes in development policies during the 1960s and 1970s. The structuralist partiality to industrialisation and large-scale capital accumulation is implicitly criticised. The way in which the alternative programmes try to stimulate the agricultural sector is completely different from the way World Bank and IMF programmes do; the alternative way does correspond with the structuralist view, though. As has been explained earlier, the World Bank and IMF programmes centre around liberalisation of prices, abolishing or restructuring marketing organisations, and abolishing tariff restrictions; the role of the government is to be restricted. The alternative programmes, however, stress that the government has an important role in stimulating agricultural growth. Moreover, promotion of the agricultural sector should not be realised at all costs. The strategy has to lead to a better income distribution and must be aimed at improving the position of peasants and women. In order to realise this, the alternative programmes argue in favour of land reforms, improvement of access to inputs for peasants and women by means of specific allocation of credit and stabilisation of agricultural prices.

Improvement of linkages between agriculture and industry

To promote rural development, the alternative programmes also pay a lot of attention to improving the relation between agricultural and non-agricultural production. Particularly in Africa, the relation between the agricultural and the industrial sector has been poorly developed (Stewart, 1994, p. 105). This has been caused by such factors as poor infrastructure, the limited use of agricultural and non-agricultural inputs produced at home, and the lack of formal credit facilities in rural areas. Due to this, profits in specific sectors are said to flow abroad. Moreover, the development of a sector is hampered by too small a capacity of other sectors. Thus an increase in agricultural production requires an increase in the use of products that need to be imported since the domestic industries do not produce these inputs. For this reason the alternative strategies set great store by improving the physical and social infrastructure, in particular in rural areas. The need to improve education in rural areas is also emphasised. Besides, the development of a labour intensive industry to process local raw materials is also argued in favour of. Government policy ought to stimulate small-scale rural and urban industries as well as the informal sector, and to this end rural credit facilities ought to be developed. Moreover, competition between large-scale industries ought to be promoted. Abolishing price controls for large industries, to prevent monopolisation, may be useful.

A policy aimed at sustainable human development

Fighting the decrease in welfare of the very poor is paramount in the alternative strategies. In particular in the report *Adjustment with a Human Face* (Cornia *et al.*, 1987) humankind is at the centre of the process of adjustment. The report states that the consequences to the most vulnerable groups in society should not be considered unimportant in the analysis of adjustment. Economic policy should be directed towards an improvement of productivity and prosperity for the poor. This means that more financial support should be provided for education and health care since these two factors provide the essential conditions for growth of productivity and political and social stability. Moreover, more institutions should be established that take care of the distribution of medications in rural areas. The humane development also requires greater equality in income distribution. It is argued that a change in the way in which incomes are realised is more important to the improvement of income distribution than redistributing incomes afterwards. To realise this, equal access to production factors is argued in favour of, and the importance of land reforms is again emphasised. Furthermore, the introduction of a system of progressive taxes on consumer goods is proposed.

An external policy aimed at selective protection and regional import substitution

The export-oriented strategy by means of abolishing tariffs, as advocated by the World Bank and the IMF, is rejected. Import restrictions to protect infant industries are considered an important means to develop the domestic industry. Cornia *et al.* (1992) explicitly state that these restrictions should be used only temporarily and in the form of tariffs, not quotas. Moreover, the restrictions should be related to sectors rather than to individual enterprises. The alternative strategies are very much in favour of instituting a regional African market. Import restrictions should not be applied at a national, but rather at a regional level. A form of regional self-reliance is actually suggested. In the above-mentioned Lagos Plan of Action, self-reliance was even the central theme. The prime objective of this plan was to found an African Economic Community, which unfortunately was a complete failure. It was the Tanzanian president Nyerere who made the notion of self-reliance widely known. It refers to one's faith in one's own strength: Africa's economic development should not be determined by Western influences. The domestic economic development should be promoted by means of protection of the domestic economy against the international economic organisation. The notion of self-reliance was strongly influenced by critical economic theories like the centre-periphery theory and the theory of unequal exchange. Both theories argue that international markets developed unfavourably for developing countries. Finally, a policy aimed at stimulating export of primary products is argued in favour of. The composition of exports should be expanded, especially by means of a specific government policy. The importance of devaluations of the currency is also pointed out. However, it is explicitly stated that it is useless to carry out devaluations without policy-related measures aimed at an increase in production capacity and a better income distribution.

8.6 Summary and conclusions

Criticism of World Bank and IMF adjustment programmes is especially directed towards the social consequences of these programmes. The critics stress that the structural adjustment programmes disastrously affect the environment and the poorest communities. Moreover, the adjustment programmes lead to a marginalisation of the position of women. The World Bank and the IMF dispute critics' arguments by pointing out that economic growth, which should be realised through the programmes, can and will involve sustained development that will not affect the environment, and that will improve the prosperity of the poor and the position of women.

Also in relation to the social consequences of the adjustment programmes one can hardly rely on empiricism. There is a great shortage of empirical studies that have thoroughly analysed the social consequences of the adjustment programmes. The studies that have been conducted show a contrasting picture. In some cases the adjustment programmes have had positive social consequences, in other cases negative ones. A better insight into the social consequences can probably be obtained only with the lapse of time. The period since the implementation of the adjustment programmes has been simply too short to draw any concrete conclusions.

In the course of time, critics have developed several alternative adjustment programmes. Despite the differences between these adjustment programmes, there are also significant similarities. All alternative adjustment programmes criticise the advantages of the free market, which the IMF and World Bank programmes centre on. The role of the government is an important one. By means of a specific policy, the government must make sure that the poorest communities are not victimised by adjustment policies. All alternative adjustment programmes feature humane development. In this context the alternative programmes point out the significance of ownership distribution. A concentration of property with a small group of people is rejected. Therefore, land reforms are considered highly important. Full liberalisation of trade policy, as considered desirable by the Bank and the IMF, is rejected in the alternative adjustment programmes. All alternative programmes stress the importance of import restrictions to protect infant industries. Besides, critics claim, all alternative adjustment programmes take into account the specific circumstances in Africa, more so than the regular IMF and World Bank programmes do. Often one opts for a policy explicitly aimed at stimulating small-scale labour-intensive agriculture and industries. If the starting-points of most alternative adjustment programmes are compared with the characteristics of a broad interpretation of the notion of structuralism – already mentioned in the introduction to this study – one will certainly discern many similarities. Thus, the alternative adjustment programmes can generally be referred to as structuralist adjustment programmes. Note that recent adjustment programmes, in comparison to the traditional structuralist theory, place greater emphasis on the importance of stimulating the agricultural sector and less on large-scale capital accumulation.

Notes

1 A well-known example of a project that gave rise to a gulf of criticism refers to the Sardar Sarovar dam. As part of this project, the World Bank funded a large-scale irrigation project in the Narmada valley in India. The aim of this project was to supply water and electricity for over 40 million people. However, a consequence of this project would be that 250,000 to 1,000,000 people would have to be evacuated from 245 villages. Moreover, the project would affect the environment considerably. After growing criticism the World Bank eventually suspended its financial support of this project.

2 For some countries the situation has deteriorated so very much during a short period of time that the reliablity of the data may be questioned.

3 With respect to Africa as a whole, 84 per cent of the poorest inhabitants lives in rural areas (Husain, 1994, Table 4.1).

4 For an analysis of the effects of adjustment programmes in Kenya (and Zimbabwe) on women, see also Driessen (1994).

5 Cummings (1992) critically analyses the LPA. Browne (1992) discusses AAF. For a summary of the most important policy elements in AAF, I refer to Abbott (1993).

9 Conclusions

This study has presented an outline of the theoretical and empirical debates on structural adjustments in Africa in the shape of a comparison between the neoliberal and the structuralist point of view. It has been shown that theoretical evidence for the World Bank and IMF adjustment programmes is based on neoliberal beliefs whereas critics of the two Bretton Woods institutions mainly refer to structuralists notions. Neoliberals and structuralists differ especially with respect to their vision of the role of the government. The neoliberals strongly believe in the perfect functioning of the market mechanism. They argue that a policy aimed at liberalising markets, privatisation, and reducing government intervention is the best way to guarantee economic growth in Africa. The neoliberal economists – and the World Bank and the IMF as well – argue that the crisis in Africa is primarily the result of a faulty government policy. According to the neoliberals, the multitude of government regulations and a policy aimed at import substitution have had disastrous consequences, especially for the agricultural sector. According to the World Bank and the IMF, growth of the agricultural sector is among the prime prerequisites for improved welfare in Africa. The structural adjustment programmes, therefore, very much concentrate on this. Despite distinct differences per country, the basic philosophy of the measures in all adjustment programmes is the same: a decrease in government intervention is paramount and should be realised by means of privatisation, abolishing price control, and a trade policy aimed at the promotion of exports.

The structuralists, however, question the advantages of a free market and stress the important role that the government plays in starting a process of economic development in Africa. According to them, the African crisis is mainly the result of certain external factors and a poor initial situation. Furthermore, critics claim that the World Bank and IMF adjustment programmes negatively affect the position of the very poorest groups of the population, the environment and women. Critics also doubt whether the structural adjustment programmes have actually stimulated economic growth. They point out, for example, the slight effects of the programmes on investment. An important reason for this is the emphasis in the programmes on the reduction of government expenditure which leads to a decrease in expenditure for infrastructure.

Many empirical studies have been conducted into the effectiveness of adjustment programmes. However, it is almost impossible to say anything about the degree to which the adjustment programmes have been successful. The outcomes per study differ to a large extent. Moreover, most studies are of such poor quality that it is not right to draw any concrete conclusions on the basis of these studies. This does indeed apply to both World Bank and IMF studies and studies conducted by their critics. The critics and the World Bank and the Fund study the effectiveness of the adjustment programmes by means of various methods. Usually groups of countries that did and countries that did not implement adjustments are compared. Another frequently applied method involves the comparison of economic results of countries before they implement an adjustment programme and economic results after an adjustment programme has been implemented. A significant problem related to both methods is that external factors are not taken into account. It is assumed rather too readily that the differences between countries or the differences before and after implementing the adjustment programmes can be fully ascribed to the programmes.

What conclusions then can be drawn after almost a decade of structural adjustments in Africa? The optimism especially by the World Bank and the IMF concerning the effects of adjustment programmes has not yet proved to be justified. Despite the structural adjustment programmes welfare in most African countries is still extremely low. There has hardly been any increase in economic growth, and the issue of poverty is still immense. By no means do I suggest that the situation would have been better without the implementation of adjustment programmes. It is obvious though that the adjustment programmes do not guarantee improved welfare, at least not in the short term. A great deal of additional efforts will have to be made before Africa outgrows its present economic crisis. More research into the precise effect of World Bank and IMF policy recommendations would be desirable. The use of simulation models to evaluate policy measures may be quite useful. Moreover, one ought to make more use of microdata, like data on enterprises, rather than using macrodata so that a better understanding of the effect of certain measures may be gained. Also, more in-depth research should be conducted into the specific circumstances in each separate country. After all, a certain measure may have positive effects in one country whereas it has negative effects in another.

What is also necessary is more research into the advantages of full versus partial liberalisation and into the sequence in which liberalisations must take place. According to welfare economics, in a world without market imperfections, complete liberalisation which relates to all sectors is preferred to gradual, partial liberalisation. The problem, however, is that the economic situation in many developing countries is characterised by the existence of all kinds of distortions. Often markets do not function perfectly due to, among other things, monopolies and external effects. In these cases it is not clear what the ideal policy would be. After all, it can be proven that if not all conditions for a Pareto-optimal situation are complied with, partial compliance is not necessarily optimal. This implies that liberalisation of certain sectors that are not troubled by market imperfections may be suboptimal if there are other sectors that are faced with market imperfections. If the market mechanism is affected by several factors, there is a danger of gradual liberalisation not having the desired effect. The theoretical solution is to eliminate all market imperfections simultaneously. In practice, however, this is often impossible. The optimal, practicable policy, therefore, requires in-depth research into the actual situation.

With respect to the order in which liberalisations have been implemented in the adjustment programmes, Toye (1994, p. 30) states that in the first stage of the adjustment programmes – with the exception of the programmes for some specific countries – little attention was paid to the sequence of the adjustments. The general idea was that stabilisation should take place before structural adjustments could be implemented. Subsequently the order became irrelevant. Generally, it may be stated that liberalisations were based on *ad hoc* decisions mainly. It was considered more important that something was actually being done, and as soon as possible too, without explicitly taking into account the ideal order of the adjustments. Naturally, lots of projects did fail due to this particular method.

On the basis of experiences, there seems to be some consensus of opinion with respect to the order in which adjustments should be implemented. It is often stated that the first step in the process of liberalisation should be the liberalisation of the domestic real economy; that is the first step should be liberalisation of the domestic market for goods and the domestic labour market. After government regulations with reference to the prices of goods and wages have been abolished, liberalisation of the domestic financial market can be started. The reason for this being that the domestic financial market affects economic growth positively only if the anticipated additional financial means that are thus made available are distributed to enterprises that are most likely to make a profit. If liberalisation of the domestic financial market takes place before the domestic market for goods has been liberalised, the additional funds may be made available for those enterprises that only seem to be profit-making. It may be that these enterprises can continue to exist only with the help of government protection. The issue whether domestic financial liberalisation ought to take place before or after liberalisation of foreign trade is not that easy to solve (see Gibson and Tsakalatos, 1994, p. 591). Economists who argue in favour of liberalisation of foreign trade before the domestic financial market has been liberalised, substantiate their point of view by stressing that the additional financial means should be distributed to enterprises that are truly viable. Liberalisation of the domestic financial market prior to trade liberalisation may result in many funds flowing to enterprises that can exist only because they are protected by trade barriers. Other economists argue that liberalisation of foreign trade can probably be successful only after the domestic financial market has been liberalised, since in that case the efficiency benefits of trade can be realised. Empirical evidence for this line of reasoning is provided by the study by Berthelemy and Varoudakis (1994), mentioned in Chapter 3. They argue that trade has a positive effect on economic growth because of a more efficient allocation of production factors. This efficient allocation of production factors can take place only if the financial system has been properly developed. Finally, in general it may be stated that the capital account cannot be liberalised until the domestic financial market has been liberalised. Liberalisation of the capital account involves the abolition of capital monitoring so that financial capital can flow in and out of a country unrestrictedly. If the capital account is liberalised before the domestic financial market has been liberalised, there is a danger of substantial capital flight since in such a situation domestic interest rates are usually kept low artificially. A simultaneous liberalisation of the capital account and the domestic financial market is also unfavourable. Domestic financial liberalisations are likely to result in an increase in domestic interest rates. If capital monitoring is abolished, a considerable foreign capital inflow may occur which will bring about an appreciation of the currency. This involves several negative consequences for export possibilities. Despite the fact that the World Bank policy in this field has improved in the course of time (Gunning, 1994, p. 45), in my opinion more attention ought to be paid to the optimal extent and the order of liberalisations in developing adjustment programmes. Again this requires further in-depth investigations into the specific circumstances in each country.

A hopeful development is that there appears to be some consensus of opinion among the World Bank and the IMF on the one hand, and their critics on the other hand. The World Bank, and to a smaller extent the IMF, increasingly take into account the social and environmental consequences of their programmes. The World Bank today even opts for sustainable development. Although the critics claim that nothing has really happened, the World Bank in particular does seem to give in to the critics' demands. The critics themselves are less extreme in rejecting liberalisation in general and an export-oriented strategy in particular. Moreover, many critics now acknowledge that complete isolation from foreign influences, which used to be argued for in the past, has negative effects. Therefore, export promotion plays an important role in recent alternative programmes. Full trade liberalisation is not argued in favour of, though – regional liberalisation is opted for – so that great emphasis is placed on developing an African market. Moreover, an explicit choice for the stimulation of exports by small-scale labour-intensive agriculture is made. The critics acknowledge that the excessive emphasis on industrialisation – of which the early structuralists used to be in favour – is not the right way to solve the African problem. The critics also state that policy measures should aim at agricultural growth.

The above by no means implies that both the critics and the World Bank and the IMF will soon agree fully on the method of implementing adjustments in Africa. Especially their view on the role of the government and the advantages of a liberalised market economy will continue to differ strongly. Despite the fact that this debate appears to become slightly more balanced, it is true that in general the points of view are extreme. The World Bank and the IMF are so very convinced that the government acts wrongly and will continue to do so, that in the adjustment programmes a disproportionately amount of attention is paid to the privatisation of public enterprises and the abolition of government intervention. However, it is not clear whether these measures do actually promote market forces. After all, adjustment policies have not been aimed mainly at creating conditions that promote well-functioning market forces (Tims, 1994, p. 173). Privatisation of public enterprises often amounts to converting a government monopoly into a private monopoly, and privatisation is of little use when there is no reliable judicial system to protect property. For markets to function properly, all participants have to be familiar with all markets and prices. Information on markets is an essential prerequisite for the functioning of markets. According to Tims (1994, p. 173), the government must play an important role in this field. Still, critics only too readily assume that the government will act correctly. To justify their argument in favour of government intervention, they frequently point out the existence of market imperfections. The market does not function well, and the government must change this by means of a particular policy. Theoretically, the critics are right in believing that the existence of market imperfections may suggest an active role for the government. However, it may well be that market imperfections which arise due to government intervention are larger than the imperfections that are brought about in a free market. In other words, government failures may well exceed market failures. Further research into the role of the government and the way in which the government should implement policy measures would be advisable with a view to improving market forces.

In addition to more attention to specific measures Africa ought to execute, it is also important that more emphasis is placed on the role of donors in adjustment programmes. First, more attention should be paid to the policy pursued within the donor countries; it should be investigated whether these policies are not in violation of the policy changes they impose on Africa. For example, arguments in favour of trade liberalisations in Africa ought to go hand in hand with completely opening up the Western markets to African products. Furthermore, more attention ought to be paid to the question whether the present conditionality is really that favourable. It is often stated that rewarding a certain adjustment policy with additional funds is necessary in order to realise a change in the policy. In principle, however, the adjustment programmes should have positive effects to the countries involved. The crucial question is whether a policy change that has positive results for the country involved should be brought about by means of additional funds. If the country is convinced about the advantages of a certain policy change, it will eventually implement this policy change without a reward to look forward to. Several recent studies argue that applying foreign funds to enforce a certain policy, may actually lead to a country implementing the change just because these funds have been promised, and not because the country itself believes in the advantages of the change in policy (see e.g. Gunning, 1994; Rodrik, 1989). Thus it is likely that the recipient will continue its earlier policy and cancel many of the enforced measures when the flow of financial means from different donors has ended. The private sector in the recipient country may anticipate this and postpone important decisions, which will naturally have social consequences (for a theoretical discussion, see e.g. Calvo, 1988). The crucial aspect here is the credibility of the liberalisations initiated by the government. If the private sector feels that the government executes policy changes merely because they receive funds from foreign donors, the credibility of the government will be affected. This may imply that it is not advisable to enforce a certain policy by means of additional financing. Of course, the additional funds may enable countries to start a certain adjustment policy if the policy changes involve social or economic costs. Moreover, the adjustment loans may be temporarily necessary until the adjustment programmes yield positive effects. It is, however, not clear which measures involve high costs and which measures are relatively cheap. In general, it is rather important to investigate which measures in the adjustment programmes lead to adjustment costs and should be financially supported for this very reason. Moreover, the extent to which the government of the recipient country is convinced that the measures are desirable ought to be determined before the adjustment loans are actually issued. An adjustment programme will be successful only if the policy designers of the recipient country assent to it. I do not mean to suggest that countries that do not fully agree with the basic World Bank and IMF policy must be excluded from foreign financial funds. I feel that in drawing up the adjustment programme one ought to take into account more the insights and needs of the adjusting countries. In practice, the World Bank and the IMF determine the adjustment programmes. The recipient governments cannot do anything but to accept what has been thought out for them. The adjustment policy is actually enforced by, among other things, excluding the country involved from additional foreign funds if it does not consent to the programme. In such a situation it is not surprising that the results are disappointing, and cancellation of the programme might be advisable. I am of the opinion that one should strive for a situation in which the adjustment programmes are designed by means of a dialogue between the World Bank and the IMF, and the recipient developing country – initially regardless of the foreign funds attached. Determining financial support by the World Bank and the IMF should not take place until all parties can accept the adjustment programmes and believe in its advantages. Perhaps this will lead less often to countries accepting adjustment programmes merely because of the additional financial means attached; moreover, it may even safeguard the continuation of the policy after the flow of financial means from donors has ended.

References

Abbott, G.C. (1993) *Debt Relief and Sustainable Development In Sub-Saharan Africa*. Glasgow: Edward Elgar.

Adams, D.W. (1991) 'Taking a Fresh Look at Informal Finance', in: P. Callier (ed.) *Financial Systems and Development in Africa*, EDI Policy Seminar. Washington, DC: World Bank, 29–43.

Addison, D. (1989) *The World Bank Revised Minimum Standard Model*, Policy, Planning and Research Working Papers, WPS 231. Washington, DC: World Bank.

Akiyama, T. and D.F. Larson (1994) *The Adding-Up Problem: Strategies for Primary Commodity Exports in Sub-Saharan Afrika*, Policy Research Working Papers, WPS 1245. Washington, DC: World Bank.

Amin, S. (1973) 'Underdevelopment and Dependence in Black Africa: Historical Origins and Contemporary Forms', *Social and Economic Studies*, 12, 177–97.

Aryeetey, E. and M. Hyuha (1991) 'The Informal Financial Sector and Markets in Africa: an Empirical Study', in: A. Chhibber and S. Fischer (eds) *Economic Reform in Sub-Saharan Africa*. Washington, DC: World Bank, 125–37.

Bakker, A.F.P. (1992) *De internationale financiële instellingen*, Serie Bank- en Effectenbedrijf no. 28. Amsterdam: Nederlands Instituut voor Bank- en Effectenbedrijf.

Balassa, B. (1982) 'Structural Adjustment Policies in Developing Economies', *World Development*, 10, 23–38.

Balassa, B. (1989) 'Outward Orientation', in H. Chenery and T.N. Srinivasan (eds) *Handbook of Development Economics*, 2. Amsterdam: North-Holland, 1645–89.

Berg, E. and D. Sherk (1994) 'The World Bank and its Environmentalist Critics', in: Bretton Woods Commission (1994) *Bretton Woods: Looking to the Future*, Conference Proceedings. Washington, DC: Bretton Woods Committee, 20–2 July, 305–22.

Berthelemy, J.C. and A. Varoudakis (1994) *Financial Development, Financial Policies and Growth*, paper presented on the workshop 'Financial Development and Economic Growth: Theory and Experiences from Developing Economies', Groningen, 7–9 December.

Bird, G. (1993) 'Sisters in Economic Development: The Bretton Woods Institutions and Developing Countries', *Journal of Economic Development*, 5, 1–25.

Bond, M. (1983) 'Agricultural Response to Price in Sub-Saharan African Countries', *IMF Staff Papers*, 30, 703–26.

Boserup, E. (1970) *Women's Role in Economic Development*. New York: St Martin's Press.

Bourguignon, J. de Melo and C. Morrisson (1991) 'Poverty and Income Distribution During Adjustment: Issues and Evidence from the OECD Project', *World Development*, 19, 1485–1508.

Bourguignon, J. de Melo and A. Suwa (1991) 'Distributional Effects of Adjustment Policies: Simulations for Archetype Economies in Africa and Latin America', *The World Bank Economic Review*, 5, 339–66.

Bourguignon, F., W.H. Branson and J. de Melo (1992) 'Adjustment and Income Distribution: A Micro-Macro Model for Counterfactual Analysis', *Journal of Development Economics*, 38, 17–39.

Bouton, L., C. Jones and M. Kiguel (1994) *Macroeconomic Reform and Growth in Africa: Adjustment in Africa Revisited*, Policy Research Working Papers, WPS 1394. Washington, DC: World Bank.

Brandon, K. (1994) 'Environment and Development at the Bretton Woods Institutions', in: Bretton Woods Commission (1994) *Bretton Woods: Looking to the Future*, Conference Proceedings. Washington, DC: Bretton Woods Committee, 20–2 July, 133–42.

Bretton Woods Commission (1994) *Bretton Woods: Looking to the Future*, Conference Proceedings. Washington, DC: Bretton Woods Committee, 20–2 July.

Browne, R.S. (1992) 'Alternative Policy Frameworks for African Development in the 1990s', in: J.E. Nyang'oro and T.M. Shaw (eds) *Beyond Structural Adjustment in Africa: The Political Economy of Sustainable and Democratic Development*. New York: Praeger, 71–83.

Bruce, C.A. and D. Ndii (1991) *Framework for Macroeconomic Analysis*, Policy, Research and External Affairs, WPS 767. Washington, DC: World Bank.

Calvo, G. (1988) 'Costly Trade Liberalizations: Durable Goods and Capital Mobility', *IMF Staff Papers*, 35, 461–73.

Chenery, H.B. and A.M. Strout (1966) 'Foreign Assistance and Economic Development', *American Economic Review*, 56, 679–735.

Chhibber, A. (1992) 'Exchange Reforms, Supply Response, and Inflation in Afrika', in: I. Goldwin and L.A. Winters, *Open Economies: Structural Adjustment and Agriculture*, CEPR. Cambridge: Cambridge University Press, 125–39.

Chirot, D. (1977) *Social Change in the Twentieth Century*. New York: Harcourt Brace Jovanovich, inc.

Claassen, E.M. (1992) 'Discussion', in: I. Goldwin and L.A. Winters, *Open Economies: Structural Adjustment and Agriculture*, CEPR. Cambridge: Cambridge University Press, 86–91.

Cornia, G.A., R. Jolly and F. Stewart (1987) *Adjustment with a Human Face*, UNICEF. Oxford: Oxford University Press.

Cornia, G.A., R van der Hoeven and T. Mkandawire (1992) 'Overview of an Alternative Long-term Development Strategy', in: G.A. Cornia, R van der Hoeven and T. Mkandawire (eds) *Africa's Recovery in the 1990s: From Stagnation and Adjustment to Human Development*, UNICEF. New York: St Martin's Press, 159–91.

Cummings, R.J. (1992) 'A Historical Perspective on the Lagos Plan of Action', in: J.E. Nyang'oro and T.M. Shaw (eds) *Beyond Structural Adjustment in Africa: The Political Economy of Sustainable and Democratic Development*. New York: Praeger, 29–47.

Davidson, D. (1993) *The Black Man's Burden: Africa and the Curse of the Nation-State*. Lagos: Spectrum Books.

Devarajan, S. and J. de Melo (1991) 'Membership in the CFA Zone: Odyssean Journey or Trojan Horse?', in: A. Chhibber and S. Fischer, *Economic Reform in Sub-Saharan Africa*. Washington, DC: World Bank, 25–34.

Devarajan, S. and D. Rodrik (1992) 'Do the Benefits of Fixed Exchange Rates Outweigh their Costs?: The CFA Zone in Africa', in: I. Goldwin and L.A. Winters (eds), *Open Economies: Structural Adjustment and Agriculture*, CEPR. Cambridge: Cambridge University Press, 66–83.

Development Committee (1991) *The Effect of Industrial Countries' Trade, Agricultural and Industrial Policies on Developing Countries*, Development Issues, 27. Washington, DC: Development Committee.

Dollar, D. (1992) 'Outward-oriented Developing Economies Really Do Grow More Rapidly: Evidence from 95 LDCs, 1976–1985', *Economic Development and Cultural Change*, 40, 523–44.

Driessen, D. (1994) *Women Rise Up Against the World Bank and the IMF: An Analysis of Strategies of Resistance to Structural Adjustment Policies in Kenya and Zimbabwe from a*

Gender Perspective, MA Thesis, Department of International Relations and Public International Law, Faculty of Political and Socio-Cultural Sciences, University of Amsterdam.

Durning, A.B. (1989) *Poverty and the Environment: Reversing the Downward Spiral*, Worldwatch Paper 92. Washington, DC: Worldwatch Institute.

Easterly, W. (1989) *A Consistency Framework for Macroeconomic Analysis*, Policy, Research and External Affairs, WPS 234. Washington, DC: World Bank.

Easterly, W., E.C. Hwa, P. Kongsamut and J. Zizek (1990) *Modeling the Macroeconomic Requirements of Policy Reforms*, Policy, Research and External Affairs, WPS 417. Washington, DC: World Bank.

ECA (Economic Commission for Africa) (1989) *African Alternative Framework to Structural Adjustment Programmes for Socio-Economic Recovery and Transformation*. Addis Ababa: ECA.

Elbadawi, I.A. (1992) *World Bank Adjustment Lending and Economic Performance in Sub-Saharan Africa in the 1980s: A Comparison of Early Adjusters, Late Adjusters, and Nonadjusters*, Policy Research Working Papers, WPS 1001. Washington, DC: World Bank.

Elbadawi, I.A. and N. Majd (1993) *Macroeconomic Framework for an Oil-Based Economy: The Case of Bahrain*, Policy, Research and External Affairs, WPS 1133. Washington, DC: World Bank.

Elbadawi, I.A. and K. Schmidt-Hebbel (1991) *Macroeconomic Structure and Policy in Zimbabwe*, Policy, Research and External Affairs, WPS 771. Washington, DC: World Bank.

Elbadawi, I.A., D. Ghura and G. Uwujaren (1992) *World Bank Adjustment Lending and Economic Performance in Sub-Saharan Africa in the 1980s: A Comparison with other Low-Income Countries*, Policy Research Working Papers, WPS 1000. Washington, DC: World Bank.

Erzan, R. and P. Svedberg (1989) *Protection Facing Exports from Sub-Saharan Afrika in the EC, Japan, and the United States*, Policy Research Working Papers, WPS 320. Washington, DC: World Bank.

Everaert, L., F. Garcia-Pinto and J. Ventura (1990) *A RMSM-X Model for Turkey*, Policy, Research and External Affairs, WPS 486. Washington, DC: World Bank.

Foroutan, F. (1993) *Trade Reform in Ten Sub-Saharan African Countries*, Policy Research Working Papers, WPS 1222. Washington, DC: World Bank.

Fry, M.J (1988) *Money, Interest, and Banking in Economic Development*. New Haven, CT: Yale University Press.

George, S. (1988) *A Fate Worse than Debt*. Harmondsworth: Penguin.

George, S. (1992) *The Debt Boomerang*. London: Pluto Press.

George, S. and F. Sabelli (1994) *Faith and Credit: The World Bank's Secular Empire*. Harmondsworth: Penguin.

Gibson, H.D. and E. Tsakalatos (1994) 'The Scope and Limits of Financial Liberalisation in Developing Countries: A Critical Survey', *Journal of Development Studies*, 40, 578–628.

Greenaway, D. and C. Milner (1993) *Trade and Industrial Policy in Developing Countries*. London: Macmillan.

Greenaway, D. and O. Morrissey (1993) 'Structural Adjustment and Liberalisation in Developing Countries: What Have We Learned?', *Kyklos*, 46, 241–61.

Guillaumont, P. and S. Guillaumont (1991) 'Exchange Rate Policies and the Social Consequences of Adjustment in Africa', in: A. Chhibber and S.Fischer, *Economic Reform in Sub-Saharan Africa*. Washington, DC: World Bank, 12–25.

Gunning, J.W. (1994) 'Structurele Aanpassing', in: Preadviezen van de Koninklijke Vereniging voor de Staathuishoudkunde 1994, *Vijftig jaar na Bretton Woods*. Utrecht: Lemma, 33–53.

Gupta, K.L. (1984) *Finance and Economic Growth in Developing Countries*. London: Croom Helm.

Gupta, K.L. and R. Lensink (1993) *Informal Credit Markets, Deregulation and Private Investment*, Research Memorandum 559. Groningen: Institute of Economic Research.

Hadjimichael, M.T., D. Ghura, M. Mühleisen, R. Nord and E.M. Uçer (1995), *Sub-Saharan Africa: Growth, Savings, and Investment, 1986–93*, IMF Occasional Paper 118. Washington, DC: IMF.

Hartog, F. (1981) *Toegepaste Welvaartstheorie*. Leiden: Stenfert Kroes.

Helleiner, G.K. (1986) 'Outward Orientation, Import Stability and African Economic Growth: an Empirical Investigation', in: S. Lall and F. Stewart (eds) *Theory and Reality in Development*. London: Macmillan, 139–53.

Hermes, N. (1992) *De Internationale Schuldencrisis*. Groningen: Wolters-Noordhoff.

Hermes, N. and R. Lensink (1992) 'The Magnitude and Determinants of Capital Flight: The Case for Six Sub-Saharan African Countries', *The Economist*, 140, 515–30.

Hirschman, A. (1958) *Strategy of Economic Development*. New Haven, CT: Yale University Press.

Honohan, P. (1990a) *Monetary Cooperation in the CFA Zone*, Policy Research Working Papers 389. Washington, DC: World Bank.

Honohan, P. (1990b) *Price and Monetary Convergence in Currency Unions: The Franc and Rand Zones*, Policy Research Working Papers 390. Washington, DC: World Bank.

Husain, I. (1993) *Trade, Aid and Investment in Sub-Saharan Africa*, Policy Research Working Papers 1214. Washington, DC: World Bank.

Husain, I. (1994) 'Does Structural Adjustment Help or Hurt the Poor?', in: L. Boer and J. Rooimans (eds) *The World Bank and Poverty Reduction*, The Hague: Ministry of Foreign Affairs, Development Cooperation Information Department.

IMF (International Monetary Fund) *Survey*, Washington, DC, several issues.

IMF (1987) *Theoretical Aspects of the Design of Fund-Supported Adjustment Programs*, Occasional Paper 55. Washington, DC: IMF.

IMF (1992) *Issues and Developments in International Trade Policy*, World Economic and Financial Surveys, August 1992. Washington, DC: IMF.

Institute for International Economics (1993) 'Rethinking the Bretton Woods: A New World System', *International Economic Insights*, 4, 5.

Jenkins, R. (1992) 'Theoretical Perspectives', in: T. Hewitt, H. Johnson and D. Wield (eds) *Industrialization and Development*. Oxford: Oxford University Press, 128–66.

Khadr, A. and K. Schmidt-Hebbel (1989) *A Framework for Macroeconomic Consistency for Zimbabwe*, Policy, Research and External Affairs, WPS 310. Washington, DC: World Bank.

Kraaij, F. van der (1994) 'Background Notes on Sub-Saharan Africa', in: R. van der Hoeven and F. van der Kraaij, *Structural Adjustment and Beyond in Sub-Saharan Africa*. London: James Currey, 240–57.

Krueger, A.O. (1978) *Foreign Trade Regimes and Economic Development: Liberalization Attempts and Consequences*. Cambridge, MA: Ballinger.

Krueger, A.O. (1985) 'Import Substitution Versus Export Promotion', *Finance and Development*, 20–3.

La Ferrara, E., G. Castillo and J. Nash (1994) *The Reform of Mechanisms for Foreign Exchange Allocation*, Policy Research Working Papers 1268. Washington, DC: World Bank.

Lele, U. (1991) 'Woman, Structural Adjustment, and Transformation: Some Lessons and Questions from the African Experience', in C.H. Gladwin (ed.) *Structural Adjustment and African Woman Farmers*. Gainesville, FL: University of Florida Press.

Lensink, R. (1993) *External Finance and Development*. Groningen: Wolters-Noordhoff.

Lensink, R. and F. Vijselaar (1995) 'Structurele Aanpassingen in Afrika ten Zuiden van de Sahara: een Overzicht', *Maandschrift Economie*, 59, 164–84.

Lewis, W.A. (1954) 'Economic Development with Unlimited Supplies of Labour', *Manchester School of Economic and Social Studies*, 22, 139–91.

Lopez, R. and D. Rodrik (1989) *Trade Restrictions with Imported Intermediate Inputs*, Policy Research Working Papers 174. Washington, DC: World Bank.

Michaely, M. (1977) 'Exports and Growth: An Empirical Investigation', *Journal of Development Economics*, 4, 49–54.

Miller, R.R. and M.A. Sumlinski (1994) *Trends in Private Investment in Developing Countries 1994*, IFC Discussion Paper, 20. Washington, DC: World Bank.

Mills, A.C. and R. Nallari (1992) *Analytical Approaches to Stabilization and Adjustment Programs*, EDI Seminar Paper 44. Washington, DC: Economic Development Institute (EDI) of the World Bank.

Miracle, M.P., D.S. Miracle and L. Cohen (1980) 'Informal Savings Mobilization in Africa', *Economic Development and Cultural Change*, 28, 701–24.

Montiel, P.J., P. Agenor and N.U. Haque (1993) *Informal Financial Markets in Developing Countries*. Oxford: Blackwell.

Mosley, P. (1991) 'Structural Adjustment: A General Overview, 1980–9', in: V.N. Balasubramanyam and S. Lall (eds) *Current Issues in Development Economics*. Hong Kong: Macmillan, 223–43.

Mosley, P. and J. Weeks (1993) 'Has Recovery Begun? "Africa's Adjustment in the 1980s" Revisited', *World Development*, 21, 1583–606.

Mosley, P., J. Harrigan and J. Toye (1991) *Aid and Power: The World Bank and Policy-based Lending, Volume 1 Analyses and Proposals*. London: Routledge.

Myint, H. (1980) *The Economics of the Developing Countries*. London: Hutchinson.

Nash, J. (1993) *Implementation of Trade Reform in Sub-Saharan Africa*, Policy Research Working Paper 1218. Washington, DC: World Bank.

Nicholson, W. (1992) *Microeconomic Theory: Basic Principles and Extensions*. New York: Dryden Press.

Nurkse, R. (1953) *Problems of Capital Formation in Underdeveloped Countries*. Oxford: Oxford University Press.

Nzomo, M. (1992) 'Beyond Structural Adjustment Programs: Democracy, Gender, Equity, and Development in Africa, with Special Reference to Kenya', in: J.E. Nyang'oro and T.M. Shaw (eds), *Beyond Structural Adjustment in Africa: The Political Economy of Sustainable and Democratic Development*. New York: Praeger, 99–117.

OAU (Organization for African Unity) (1980) *The Lagos Plan of Action for the Economic Development of Africa, 1980–2000*. Lagos: OAU.

OECD (Organization for Economic Co-operation and Development) (1993) *Financing and External Debt of Developing Countries*, 1992 survey. Paris: OECD.

Opschoor, J.B. (1994) 'De Bretton Woods-instellingen en het milieu', in: Preadviezen van de Koninklijke Vereniging voor de Staathuishoudkunde 1994, *Vijftig jaar na Bretton Woods*. Utrecht: Lemma, 93–119.

Pischke, J.D. Von, D. Adams, and G. Donald (1983) *Rural Financial Markets in Developing Countries*. Baltimore, MD: Johns Hopkins University Press.

Polak, J.J. (1957) 'Monetary Analysis of Income Formation and Payments Problems', *IMF Staff Papers*, 4, 1–50.

Polak, J.J. (1991) *The Changing Nature of IMF Conditionality*, Princeton Essays in International Finance no. 184. Princeton, NJ.

Prebisch, R. (1950) *The Economic Development of Latin America and its Principal Problems*. New York: Economic Commission for Latin America, United Nations.

Reed, D. (ed.) (1992) *Structural Adjustment and the Environment*. London: Earthscan Publications.

Rodrik, D. (1989) 'Credibility of Trade Reform: a Policy Maker's Guide', *The World Economy*, 12, 1–16.

Roemer, M. and S.C. Radelet (1991) 'Macroeconomic Reform in Developing Countries', in D.W. Perkins and M. Roemer (eds) *Reforming Economic Systems in Developing Countries*. Cambridge, MA: Harvard University Press, 56–80.

Rosenstein-Rodan, P.N. (1943) 'Problems of Industrialization in Eastern and Southeastern Europe', *Economic Journal*, 53, 429–39.

Rotberg, E. (1994) 'The Financial Operations of the World Bank', in: *Bretton Woods: Looking to the Future*, Commission Report Staff Review Background Papers. Washington, DC: Bretton Woods Commission, 185–214.

Schadler, S., F. Rozwadowski, S. Tiwari and D.O. Robinson (1993) *Economic Adjustment in Low-Income Countries: Experience Under the Enhanced Structural Adjustment Facility*, IMF Occasional Paper 106. Washington, DC: IMF.

Schultz, T.W. (1964) *Transforming Traditional Agriculture*. New Haven, CT: Yale University Press.

Serven, L. (1990) *A RMSM-X Model for Chile*, Policy, Research and External Affairs, WPS 508. Washington, DC: World Bank.

Stewart, F. (1994) 'Are Adjustment Policies in Africa Consistent with Long-Run Development Needs', in: W. van der Geest (ed.) *Negotiating Structural Adjustment in Africa*. London: James Currey, 99–115.

Stewart, F., S. Lall and S. Wangwe (1991) *Alternative Development Strategies in Sub-Saharan Africa*. London: Macmillan.

Svedberg, P. (1991) 'The Export Performance of Sub-Saharan Africa', *Economic Development and Cultural Change*, 39, 549–64.

Szirmai, A. (1994) *Ontwikkelingslanden: Dynamiek en Stagnatie*. Groningen: Wolters-Noordhoff.

Tarp, F. (1993) *Stabilization and Structural Adjustment: Macro-economic Frameworks for Analysing the Crisis in Sub-Saharan Africa*. London: Routledge.

Taube, G. (1993) 'Social Dimensions of Adjustment (SDA)', *Afrika Spectrum*, 2, 165–83.

Taylor, L. (1993) *Stabilization, Adjustment and Reform*, paper presented at the International Policy Workshop on International Capital Flows and Economic Adjustment in Developing Countries, Institute of Social Studies, The Hague, 2–3 December.

Tims, W. (1994) 'De Wereldbank en de Armen: Sociale Dimensies in Ontwikkelingsbeleid', in: Preadviezen van de Koninklijke Vereniging voor de Staathuishoudkunde 1994, *Vijftig jaar na Bretton Woods*. Utrecht: Lemma, 151–95.

Todaro, M.P. (1994) *Economic Development*, fifth edition. London: Longman.

Toye, J. (1994) 'Structural Adjustment: Context, Assumptions, Origin and Diversity', in: R. van der Hoeven and F. van der Kraaij (eds), *Structural Adjustment and Beyond in Sub-Saharan Africa*. London: James Currey, 18–35.

UN (United Nations) (1989) *African Economic and Financial Data*. Washington, DC: UN Development Program and the World Bank.

UN (1990) *Human Development Report 1990*. Oxford: Oxford University Press.

UN (1994) *Human Development Report 1994*. Oxford: Oxford University Press.

Vickers, J. (1991) *Woman and the World Economic Crisis*. London: Zed Books.

Wai, U.T. (1977) 'A Revisit to Interest Rates Outside the Organized Money Markets of Underdeveloped Countries', *Banca Nazionale Del Lavoro*, 2, 291–312.

Williams, M. (1994) *International Economic Organisations and the Third World*. London: Harvester Wheatsheaf.

WCED (World Commission on Environment and Development) (1987) *Our Common Future*. Oxford: Oxford University Press.

World Bank (1988) *Adjustment Lending: An Evaluation of Ten Years of Experience*, Policy and Research Series 1. Washington, DC: World Bank.

World Bank (1989) *Sub-Saharan Africa: From Crisis to Sustainable Growth*. Washington, DC: World Bank.

World Bank (1990a) *Trends in Developing Economies 1990*. Washington, DC: World Bank.

World Bank (1990b) *Adjustment Lending Policies For Sustainable Growth*, Policy and Research Series 14. Washington, DC: World Bank.

World Bank (1992a) *Adjustment Lending and Mobilization of Private and Public Resources for Growth*, Policy and Research Series 22. Washington, DC: World Bank.

World Bank (1992b) *Annual Report*. Washington, DC: World Bank.

World Bank (1992c) *Effective Implementation: Key to Development Impact*. Washington, DC: World Bank.

World Bank (1993a) *World Development Report 1993*. Washington, DC: World Bank.

World Bank (1993b) *World Tables 1993*. Washington, DC: World Bank.

World Bank (1993c) *World Debt Tables: External Finance for Developing Countries*, 1 and 2. Washington, DC: World Bank.
World Bank (1994a) *Adjustment in Africa: Reforms, Results, and the Road Ahead*. Oxford: Oxford University Press.
World Bank (1994b) *World Development Report 1994*. Washington, DC: World Bank.

Subject index

Author index